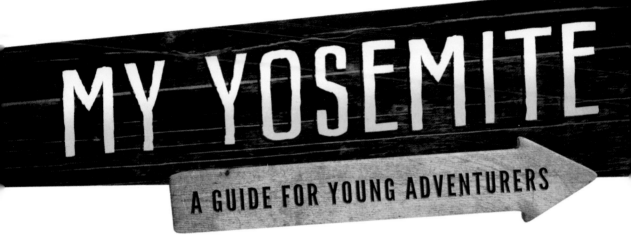

MY YOSEMITE

A GUIDE FOR YOUNG ADVENTURERS

MY YOSEMITE

A GUIDE FOR YOUNG ADVENTURERS

MIKE GRAF

ILLUSTRATIONS BY

ANNETTE FILICE

Yosemite Conservancy
Yosemite National Park

The publisher wishes to thank the S.D. Bechtel, Jr. Foundation
for the generous grant that made this book possible.

Text copyright © 2012 by Mike Graf
Maps and illustrations copyright © 2011 by Yosemite Conservancy
Additional credits can be found on pages 161–166

yosemiteconservancy.org

Yosemite Conservancy's Mission
Providing for Yosemite's future is our passion. We inspire people to
support projects and programs that preserve and protect Yosemite
National Park's resources and enrich the visitor experience.

Library of Congress Cataloging-in-Publication Data

Graf, Mike.
 My Yosemite : a guide for young adventurers / Mike Graf ; illustrations
by Annette Filice.
    p. cm.
 1. Yosemite National Park (Calif.)--Juvenile literature. 2. Yosemite
National Park (Calif.)--Guidebooks--Juvenile literature. I. Filice, Annette,
ill. II. Title.
 F868.Y6G728 2012
 979.4'47--dc23
                                        2011019204

ISBN 978-1-930238-30-5

Cover Art: *the*Bookdesigners
Book Design: *the*Bookdesigners

Illustrations by Annette Filice. Additional graphic
elements supplied by *the*Bookdesigners.

Printed in Singapore by Imago, December 2011.

1 2 3 4 5 6 – 17 16 15 14 13 12

CONTENTS

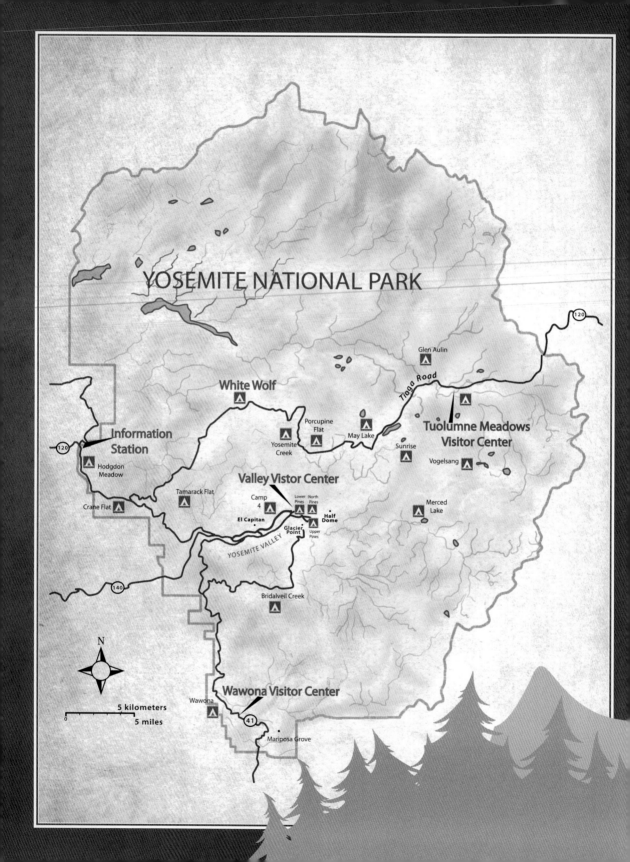

1 WELCOME TO THE BEST!

Yosemite National Park has been called "Nature's Grand Cathedral." What makes Yosemite so special? And why do nearly four million people from all over the world visit the park each year? For many, it's the amazing collection of waterfalls. Some of the tallest on the planet are here.

For others it's the massive sequoia trees. One walk among these giants and you'll see why so many visitors have been awed by their majesty. It could also be the park's incredible rocks and cliffs: in some places, over three thousand feet of sheer granite wall. And there are those who come to see a landscape created by glaciers. In the ancient past, these massive sheets of ice gouged out Yosemite Valley and its lesser-known neighbor, Hetch Hetchy Valley. There is also the high country, with its grassy meadows, spired peaks, and miles of wilderness beckoning to be explored. Of course, some people are intrigued by Yosemite's unique history, that of the American Indians, the more recent European American past, and the famous conservationist John Muir. Read on, then explore and discover what makes Yosemite special for you.

The Best Things to See: Insider Tips

"The towering waterfalls of Yosemite National Park are some of the main attractions that drew me here. I like to take the time and hike to the waterfalls and the beautiful scenery that cannot always be seen from the road. The key is to get out of your comfort zone and go a little further. The hikes to these waterfalls are awe-inspiring and definitely worth it."

—SUZIE GUTIERREZ, Yosemite Park Ranger

"I love being up above treeline, in the land of the pikas and bighorn sheep. Camping at a high alpine lake and watching as the first rays of sun light up the tops of the surrounding cirques is the best gift I can imagine."

—SARAH STOCK, Yosemite Wildlife Biologist

"My favorite part of the park is Yosemite Valley. I've never seen anything else in my travels that's more beautiful. Even though it's crowded in the summer you can still find quiet spots away from the roadways, and if you walk around at night, especially on a moonlit night, you can follow paved paths that were congested just a few hours earlier, and find solitude and connect with all that granite rising around you while everyone else is asleep. It's just you, the night, and eternity. Oh, and maybe a few bears..."

—SHELTON JOHNSON, Yosemite Park Ranger

"My favorite part of the park is Tuolumne Meadows. It is less traveled and so pristine and beautiful. I used to work up there, and while on my break, I would hoof it to the top of Lembert Dome and have my lunch. The views from up there are amazing. You get an incredible panorama of the Sierra and all the way down toward the valley. Also, the vast Tuolumne Meadows are spread out right below. It's just such an incredible vista of open space."

—KARI COBB, Yosemite Park Ranger

DID YOU KNOW?

Yosemite became a national park on October 1, 1890, the third national park in the United States. The first two were Yellowstone in 1872 and Sequoia on September 25, 1890.

PLANNING YOUR VISIT ➡

Getting Started

YOSEMITE GUIDE: A seasonally updated park newspaper is given out free at the park's entrance gates and visitor centers. It has news about activities, programs, hikes, and other events going on throughout the park. The newspaper includes a map and information on park buses, their schedules, and where to catch them, as well as places to eat and stay. It is a great way to get oriented when you first arrive.

THE VISITOR CENTER: You might want to start your adventure in Yosemite National Park at the Yosemite Valley Visitor Center. There are maps, books, exhibits, and rangers on hand to answer all of your questions. The visitor center also has a wealth of displays, on the geology of Yosemite, glaciers, granite formation, Half Dome, forest and plant zones and the wildlife within them, giant sequoias, Yosemite people of the past, and famous Yosemite artists, among other topics. There are also visitor centers at Wawona, Big Oak Flat, Tuolumne Meadows, and Lee Vining.

PANORAMIC VIEWS: Yosemite has many famous viewpoints that offer sweeping vistas of the park's landscapes. Perhaps the two most talked about are Tunnel View and Glacier Point. From these two spots you can glimpse a great deal of the grand scenery you are about to spend time in. Olmsted Point, on Tioga Road, is another great viewpoint, overlooking the back of Half Dome with a panorama of glacier-sculpted granite all the way up to Cloud's Rest. And Sentinel Bridge in the Yosemite Valley is famous for its unobstructed view of Half Dome.

A MARMOT AT OLMSTED POINT

GO SEE IT! The very popular movie *The Spirit of Yosemite* plays every thirty minutes at the Yosemite Valley Visitor Center. This is a great way to get to know more about the awe-inspiring place you are about to visit.

Things You'll Need

Yosemite campers and hikers need to plan for weather and terrain. Here are the suggested supplies to bring:

WATER: Hikers need lots of water, at least two sixteen-ounce containers per person for most short hikes. Double this amount of water per person for longer hikes and warm weather—which is when most people hike in Yosemite. Some hikers also carry filters so they can drink water from streams near trails.

CLOTHING: Summer mornings in Yosemite often start cool but quickly warm up. Bring layers of clothes for this. Lightweight, quick-dry jackets are recommended. Rainproof or waterproof jackets are also suggested in case of summer showers. Many trails near waterfalls get quite wet and slippery, especially early in the season—waterproof shoes really help.

SHOES: Basic sneakers work for some walks in the valley. Some people like lightweight trail or running shoes on longer or steeper hikes. Also consider hiking boots for proper grip on slick granite surfaces and ankle support on rocky terrain.

FOOD: Foods high in protein and carbohydrates provide energy for long hikes. Carbohydrate-rich foods include breads, cereals, and pastas. Consider eating these the night before a big hike and having a proper breakfast. Bring lots of extra high-energy foods for the trail, too.

OTHER GEAR: Sunscreen, sunglasses, a hat, and insect repellant. Also, don't forget basic emergency items, such as a flashlight and first aid supplies, in case someone gets injured or lost or you return later than expected. You might also consider: water filters (for longer hikes); a GPS device; a whistle; your camera and extra batteries; a walking stick; extra socks; binoculars; work gloves (for climbing the cables at Half Dome); Band-Aids or moleskin; and aspirin.

GETTING TO YOSEMITE AND GETTING AROUND

Climate Zones

Yosemite elevations range from around 1,800 feet to over 13,000 feet. The lowest part of the park is on the western side, near the town of El Portal. The highest point is 13,114 feet, at the top of Mt. Lyell, at the eastern edge of the park. Because of the huge differences in elevation, Yosemite has several climate zones and a variety of plants that grow within them.

FOOTHILLS: At the western end of the park, elevations range from 1,800 to 3,000 feet. This grassy region is hot and dry in the summer and there is little or no winter snow. Plants you can see here include manzanita, blue oak, live oak, and gray pine.

LOWER MONTANE FORESTS: Starting at around 3,000 feet, Yosemite has hot, dry summers and cool, wet winters with some snow. Many kinds of plants grow in these forested parts of the park, called lower montane forests. Trees you'll see growing here include black oak, gray pine, ponderosa pine, incense cedar, and white fir. Giant sequoia groves are also in this zone in the highest areas, near 6,000 feet.

UPPER MONTANE FORESTS: Ranging from 6,000 to 8,000 feet, these higher-elevation areas get short summers and cold, wet, snowy winters. Snow may fall beginning in November and stay on the ground until June. In this region you'll see groves of red fir, lodgepole pine, and Jeffrey pine. There are also some meadows filled with wildflowers in this zone.

SUBALPINE: From 8,000 feet to 9,500 feet the overall climate is cool to cold. Long, snowy winters and a short summer growing season are the norm. Here are subalpine forests of western white pine, mountain hemlock, and lodgepole pine. There are also subalpine wildflowers.

ALPINE: From 9,500 feet and up is the alpine zone. This zone is mostly above "treeline," the elevation where trees don't grow, due to the long, cold, and harsh winters. Much of this area is also rocky, with little soil and only small, stunted plants. Yosemite park rangers are currently taking an inventory of the plants at these high-mountain elevations in the park to see if they are being affected by global climate change.

SMITH PEAK

DID YOU KNOW?

It's cooler higher up! To know what temperature to expect at higher elevations, a general rule is to take the temperature where you are—say, 80 degrees in the valley—and subtract about 4 degrees for every thousand feet of elevation gain. That would make it around 62 degrees at Tuolumne Meadows at the same time. The same thing happens at night. A 50-degree morning in Yosemite Valley translates to around 32 degrees in the meadows—and that means frost!

YOSEMITE FALLS SEEN
FROM COOK'S MEADOW

Regions

Each region of Yosemite has unique things to offer. Here are some key areas to consider visiting:

YOSEMITE VALLEY: Almost all Yosemite visitors come to the valley, and for good reason! There is so much dramatic scenery concentrated in a small area. There are the views of Half Dome and the 3,593-foot El Capitan, and there are the waterfalls cascading and plunging down from the cliffs far above. The valley also has a unique history, from the American Indians who lived in the valley for thousands of years to John Muir and Galen Clark, who began the national park movement. Yosemite Valley is also the center of the park. It is a good place to get food and put all your gear in order for your adventures.

GLACIER POINT: Over 3,000 feet above the valley is the sheer-walled perch of Glacier Point. From this vantage point, easily reached by car or bus, you can gaze down into the valley and see the cliffs, waterfalls, and meadows. Glacier Point also offers vistas into the park's high

VIEW OF HALF DOME
FROM GLACIER POINT

country and what feels like an eye-level view of the most famous rock formation in the park, Half Dome.

SEQUOIAS IN THE MARIPOSA GROVE

WAWONA: Wawona is the gateway to the largest sequoia grove in the park, the Mariposa Grove. This region also has the Pioneer History Center, where you can step back in time and walk among historic structures. While you are there you can visit the rustic Wawona Hotel, a national historic landmark built in 1876, where you will find a visitor center and art studio dedicated to the Yosemite and California artist Thomas Hill. Finally, there are the Chilnualna Falls, less famous than those of the Yosemite Valley but certainly impressive.

TIOGA ROAD: Tioga Road is a grand traverse across the park's high country. You'll pass lakes, domes, and views of pinnacle-shaped peaks. Also along the way are the Tuolumne Grove of sequoias and many trailheads leading into the park's famous wilderness.

ALONG TIOGA ROAD

TUOLUMNE MEADOWS

TUOLUMNE MEADOWS: Here is the largest meadow in Yosemite, a gateway to hiking in the high country. The Tuolumne River runs through the meadows and gurgles and sparkles along its course through lush green grasses and wildflowers surrounded by mountain peaks and plentiful granite domes.

HETCH HETCHY: The reservoir that fills Hetch Hetchy Valley gives the city of San Francisco its drinking water. You can walk across the dam and take a drink from the always running water fountain, but swimming is not allowed. Once across, walk through the tunnel and into the Hetch Hetchy wilderness. Here you will also find several impressive waterfalls, and massive rock formations as you hike along the water's edge.

HETCH HETCHY RESERVOIR

GO SEE IT! In Yosemite Valley you can take a two-hour tram tour. The tour showcases famous sites as well as the history, geology, and plants and animals of the valley. The tram is open-aired (weather permitting) and rangers take you to the best views and other special locations. Tickets are available for the tour at activity desks at any of the lodges.

Getting There—Four Routes to Choose

There are four highways into Yosemite National Park. Each has unique features along the way.

HIGHWAY 120: Also known as the Big Oak Flat Road, this highway wanders up from oak-studded foothills and gold rush towns into the park. Once inside the Yosemite boundary you quickly pass the Hodgdon Meadow campground turnoff and, soon after, the trailhead to the Merced Grove of sequoias. Look for glimpses of Half Dome as the road approaches Yosemite Valley and then drops down, passing the 1,700-foot plunge of water known as Cascade Creek before reaching the valley floor and the Merced River.

HIGHWAY 140: This highway, which leads to the Arch Rock Entrance, is at the lowest elevation of any route into the park and is the one most often snow-free in winter. Once through the gateway towns of Mariposa and El Portal, the road passes several waterfalls and parallels the Merced River into the Yosemite Valley. Highway 140 has the added bonus of being along the YARTS (Yosemite Area Regional Transit System) route, so taking this highway gives you the option of getting into the park without your car.

HIGHWAY 41: Highway 41 leads to the South Entrance and is the road to the Wawona area and the Mariposa Grove of big trees. This road is most famous for its Tunnel View. After you drive through the tunnel, you can pull over at the turnoff and gaze into Yosemite Valley and commanding views of Half Dome, El Capitan, and Bridalveil Fall.

TIOGA ROAD: Highway 120 from the eastern side of the park enters Yosemite over a pass at 9,943 feet elevation, so it is only open in summer and early fall. This great alternative for getting to Yosemite allows you to enter within the park's beautiful high country and the Tuolumne Meadows area.

TIOGA ROAD

GO SEE IT! The Tunnel View on Highway 41 might be the most popular view in the park. Once you are there, gaze at Yosemite Valley, its sheer cliffs, and Bridalveil Fall cascading down, off in the distance.

WEATHER

One of the best times to come to the park is in late spring or early summer, when waterfalls are full. You might also want to camp in summer, when the weather typically is warm and dry. Yosemite Valley, at 4,000 feet elevation, has beautiful foliage in the fall, snow in the winter, and rushing water from snowmelt in spring. But if you venture higher up in the park, the weather is very different. Tuolumne Meadows is at more than twice the valley's elevation, around 8,600 feet. Summer temperatures are typically 10 to 20 degrees cooler there. This is not the only difference between the climates of these two areas. It snows up in Tuolumne much more often in winter, and summer thunderstorms are also more likely. In fact, hail and even snow can fall around the meadows in summer, so be prepared!

Average Temperature and Precipitation

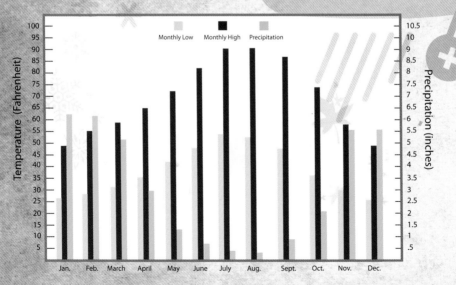

KEEPING YOSEMITE GREEN

With so many people wanting to see its beauty, Yosemite gets crowded. The result can be a lot of traffic within the park, especially during peak season. This causes pollution within the valley. However, there are some simple ways for you to reduce congestion, and by doing so you help green the park.

TAKE THE BUS! Yosemite Valley has free shuttle buses running year-long from 7 a.m. until 10 p.m., making major stops at Curry Village, Yosemite Falls, Happy Isles, and throughout the valley. During summer buses come every five to ten minutes. In winter buses stop at each location, but about thirty minutes apart. For more information on bus schedules and routes see the park newspaper, the Yosemite Valley Visitor Center, or the information posted at any one of the valley's bus stops. In addition there are free buses from the valley to Badger Pass for snow activities in winter and along the Tuolumne Meadows area for hiking in summer. There are also Glacier Point tour and hiker buses from the valley and one as well to Tuolumne Meadows. The Wawona area has free buses taking visitors to the Mariposa Grove of sequoias, or into the valley and back. The YARTS (Yosemite Area Regional Transportation System) runs buses to trailheads and other locations in and out of the park, for hikers, backpackers, and others traveling to and from Yosemite.

REUSE, REDUCE, AND RECYCLE: Try to reuse items such as water bottles, plates, bags, and containers as much as possible. Rather than using a disposable item, consider purchasing one that will last, instead. The park is full of recycling bins—use them.

SAVE ENERGY: Use a generator sparingly while in camp. This saves emissions and fuel. If you are staying in a lodge, remember to turn off the lights when you are not in the room—and don't let the water run when you're brushing your teeth.

"IT IS BY FAR THE **GRANDEST** OF ALL THE SPECIAL TEMPLES OF NATURE THAT I WAS EVER PERMITTED TO ENTER."

—JOHN MUIR

2 YOSEMITE'S RICH PAST

Many people have shaped the history of Yosemite as we know it today. From the first people of the park to explorers and conservationists, this chapter tells of Yosemite's rich past.

NATIVE YOSEMITE

Yosemite's First Name

American Indians, Miwok and Paiute, lived in the area now known as Yosemite National Park for thousands of years before the arrival of whites. The people who lived in the Yosemite Valley were called the "Ahwahneechee," after the Miwok name for the valley, "Awahnee," or gaping mouth, which describes the arrangement of the valley's walls. "Yosemite" comes from another Miwok word that means "some of them are killers." This is how Miwok people who lived outside the Yosemite area referred to the people who lived here.

An American Indian house in Yosemite Valley

Living off the Land

Every year the American Indians of Yosemite burned grasses and other plants in the valley to make the land more open. This allowed black oaks to grow and thrive and produce more acorns. Up to 60 percent of the diet of most American Indians who lived in California came from acorns. Besides fish, deer, and other animal foods, native foods of the area included pine nuts, certain flower bulbs and flower seeds, greens such as clover and miner's lettuce, and berries. The Yosemite Indians made a drink from manzanita berries, and plants were also used for tea and medicine.

There are about forty known locations in the valley where American Indians lived or camped, including at the foot of Royal Arches, near the mouth of Indian Canyon, and near Yosemite Falls. In the winter people left some of these areas and went to lower, less snowy elevations. American Indians at Yosemite used what the land provided. They used the bulb of the soaproot plant for soap and made brushes from its fibrous covering. They wove baskets from willows, maples, redbud, and other trees as well as grasses and ferns. Bows were made from cedar and dogwood. Homes were made from cedar bark.

JULIA PARKER WEAVING
IN YOSEMITE VALLEY, 1960

Julia Parker
AND THE YOSEMITE PEOPLE

Julia Parker, Kashaya Pomo and Coast Miwok, lives in the Yosemite region, as she has for over sixty years. She first came to the park in 1947, when she was sixteen. She has been working in Yosemite for so long, she says, that she "feels like Half Dome up there." Julia Parker is an expert basket weaver and she has been honored by the Smithsonian Institution for her skills. One of her goals is to pass on the stories of Yosemite's Miwok and Paiute cultures to younger generations, or to be, as she says, a "carrier of the baskets." Most times you can find her leading walks that explore native life within Yosemite, or demonstrating basket weaving, doll making, bead making, and other skills inside the Yosemite Indian museum.

JULIA PARKER ACCEPTING AN AWARD AT THE
FOR ALL MY RELATIONS CONFERENCE, 2009

The Legends of the Past

Many fascinating legends show how aware the American Indians who lived in Yosemite were of the special features of the region. One legend tells of a woman named Tiseyak who lived far down the Merced River, out of the mountains. Having quarreled with her husband, she ran east, creating the course of the river and causing oak trees and other plants to spring up along her route. Her husband caught her and they fought some more. Tiseyak was carrying a baby and cradle, and they were thrown across the canyon during the fight. They can still be seen today within the Royal Arches. Another basket she had with her landed higher up and is now called Basket Dome, or North Dome. Half Dome was also referred to as "Tis-se'-yak" by Yosemite's Ahwahneechees. Translated, this means "face of a young woman stained with tears."

In another legend, El Capitan was originally a small rock. A bear went to sleep on top of it with her two cubs. In the morning when they awoke, the rock had grown to a steep height. Neither they nor the people of the village knew how to get the bears down. So an inchworm wormed his way up the cliff, but by the time he made it to the top, he only found the starved bears' bones—although in some versions, he rescues the cubs. An ancient belief holds that both Yosemite Falls and Bridalveil Fall are inhabited by two spirits named Poloti and Pohono. They cause gusts of wind that whirl around the falls if one gets too close.

GO SEE IT! The Yosemite Museum and the reconstructed Indian Village of Ahwahnee are located just west of the Yosemite Valley Visitor Center. The museum has displays of large Miwok and Paiute baskets, traditional dress, and artifacts showing how villagers lived at Yosemite. Sound recordings and a self-guided trail that takes you to a ceremonial roundhouse in the village, a sweathouse, a bark home, a chief's house, and an acorn granary enhance your experience.

CONFLICTS AND CONSERVATION

Violence against American Indians

It wasn't until 1833, well before California's gold rush, that European Americans first made contact with the Yosemite Indians. At the start there didn't appear to be any hostility. In the late 1840s, however, conflicts occurred between miners looking for gold in the Sierra Nevada foothills and Indians of the region. By 1851 US troops were burning Indian villages and taking their food. Then two miners were killed at Bridalveil Meadows. Shortly after this, the Mariposa Battalion killed five Ahwahneechee men.

In 1853 Chief Tenaya took his people away from the violence, intending to live among the Paiutes in eastern California. His group was soon captured and forced to live on a reservation in the San Joaquin Valley. Despite all this, some returned and remained in Yosemite Valley all the way into the 1960s. Then the National Park Service stopped allowing people who aren't employees to live in the park. After that the remaining houses, which were in poor condition, were burned down in a firefighting practice session.

Tourism and the Rush to Protect Yosemite

"There was water shooting out over precipices that appeared more than a mile high," an American explorer commented in 1833 when he saw Yosemite's Valley's grandeur for the first time. His group, led by Joseph "Snowshoe" Walker, went across the Sierra Nevada, crossing the Merced and Tuolumne Rivers along the way.

"The grandeur of the scene was but softened by the haze that hung over the valley—light as gossamer—and by the clouds which partially dimmed the higher cliffs and mountains. This obscurity of vision but increased the awe with which I beheld it, and as I looked a peculiar exalted sensation seemed to fill my whole being, and I found myself in tears with emotion." Lafayette Houghton Bunnell wrote this eighteen years later, on March 27, 1851, while viewing the valley from what is now called Old Inspiration Point (near the current Tunnel View site). Bunnell was a member of the battalion that was pursuing American Indians in Yosemite. The group camped that night on the valley floor and decided to call the area "Yos s e' meti," a Miwok word for the people who lived there.

In 1855 James Hutchings led the first tourist parties into the valley. He began publicizing its beauty, writing articles on the scenery. Two of Hutchings's early visitors, Milton and Houston Mann, built the first toll road into the valley, and hotels and trails were soon developed. Thousands of tourists began flocking to the area. This prompted a drive for the government to protect its natural beauty. On June 30, 1864, at the height of the Civil War, President Lincoln signed the Yosemite Grant, deeding Yosemite Valley and the Mariposa Grove of Giant Sequoias to the people of California. This was the first time in United States history that an area of land was successfully set aside for protection.

> "THOUSANDS OF TIRED, NERVE-SHAKEN, OVER-CIVILIZED PEOPLE ARE BEGINNING TO FIND OUT THAT GOING TO THE MOUNTAINS IS GOING HOME; THAT WILDNESS IS NECESSITY; THAT MOUNTAIN PARKS AND RESERVATIONS ARE USEFUL... AS FOUNTAINS OF LIFE."

—JOHN MUIR

John Muir: Yosemite's Most Famous Advocate

John Muir, then a young man, first arrived in Yosemite in 1868. He was in search of a wild place and found Yosemite a perfect fit. Muir kept returning to Yosemite for the next forty years and eventually became the most influential naturalist of his time.

Born in Scotland in 1838, Muir had begun to love nature when he was young. His restless, adventurous spirit led him to take a thousand-mile walk from Indiana to Florida in 1867 with no planned route, other than to go by the "wildest, leafiest, and least trodden way I could find." After reaching Florida, Muir eventually booked a trip to California. He arrived in San Francisco in March 1868 and immediately headed for Yosemite—a place he had only heard about. Once Muir saw the valley for the first time, he was overwhelmed, jumping around from flower to flower and whooping it up around cliffs and waterfalls.

Muir returned to the area in 1869, carrying his tattered blue journal. He drew sketches of the scenery, climbed mountains, and became well-known in the valley for his skills as a guide and for being a great storyteller. Besides seeing Yosemite, tourists who came to the area in those days made sure they also got to meet John Muir.

Muir worked as a shepherd in Yosemite's high country when he first got to the Sierra Nevada, and he saw firsthand the problems sheep were causing. Calling them "hoofed locusts," he wrote about the grazing sheep that were trampling Yosemite's meadows. In 1889 he began a campaign to protect all of Yosemite and end grazing there. Today, driving through Tuolumne Meadows on a spring day, you can see the lush, green grasses and abundant streams and understand why Muir felt so passionate about saving the meadows.

On October 1, 1890, Congress set aside forested lands in the Yosemite area as a national park. But the valley and Mariposa Grove were still deeded to California. Muir then helped establish the Sierra Club in 1892, serving as the club's first president and working to extend the park's protection. He said he wanted to "make the mountains glad." His passion for Yosemite's scenery naturally led to an interest in the region's geology. He was certain that glaciers had carved out a great deal of the Sierra Nevada, and finding an active glacier in Yosemite's high country, below Merced Peak, convinced him even more. But Muir also loved the plants and all other aspects of nature. He made several plant surveys of the area, sketching and identifying plants both rare and common.

John Muir wrote many things about the beauty of the Yosemite area and his writings and letters helped lead to the preservation of other famous western parks, including Sequoia, Mount Rainier, Petrified Forest, and the Grand Canyon. Many places are named after Muir, including Muir Woods National Monument and Muir Beach in California, Muir Glacier in Alaska, and the 211-mile John Muir Trail from the Yosemite Valley to the summit of Mt. Whitney.

Muir became so influential that President Theodore Roosevelt accompanied him to the park, where they spent a famous night camped at Glacier Point in 1903. When you stand at Glacier Point now, you can imagine how impressed with the scenery the two conservationists were. Muir wanted to make the whole area a "Grand National Park." He convinced Roosevelt that in order to guarantee protection for Yosemite, all of it would have to be under control of the federal government, and in 1906 the park became complete, with Yosemite Valley and the Mariposa Grove transferred into it.

TEDDY ROOSEVELT AND JOHN MUIR AT GLACIER POINT

GO SEE IT! Actor Lee Stetson portrays John Muir live in stage shows at the Yosemite Theater throughout the summer. You can also learn more about John Muir at the displays in the Yosemite Valley Visitor Center. The LeConte Memorial Lodge in the valley, run by the Sierra Club, has books on Muir and a quiet reading room.

JOHN MUIR THEATER

AN INTERVIEW WITH ACTOR AND MUIR SCHOLAR
LEE STETSON

Q: WHEN DID YOU FIRST COME TO YOSEMITE AND START PERFORMING?

A: My first trip to Yosemite was in 1982. I wanted to research the life of John Muir to write a script. I first saw the valley by moonlight at Columbia Point on the Yosemite Falls trail and immediately fell in love with the scenery. I did end up writing five scripts based on Muir's life and my first performance was in 1983—coincidentally, on John Muir's birthday, April 21.

Q: WHAT MADE PERFORMING THE LIFE OF JOHN MUIR SO SPECIAL TO YOU?

A: After learning more and more about Muir and the John Muir Trail, I became increasingly intrigued by his environmental crusade. He was the father of our national parks and an original founder of the Sierra Club. But what struck me most about Muir was his amazing ability to write passionately and poetically.

Q: WHAT IS YOUR BACKGROUND IN THEATER AND STAGE?

A: I first started acting when I was twenty-eight years old. I have performed Shakespeare—*Romeo and Juliet*—and *The Crucible,* as well as around fifty major stage productions. I was also in several episodes of the TV show *Hawaii Five-0*—all this, of course, before coming to Yosemite.

Q: WHAT DO YOU THINK WOULD BE JOHN MUIR'S MESSAGE TODAY TO CHILDREN AND YOUNG ADULTS WHO VISIT THE PARK?

A: Keep engaging in and enjoying wilderness wherever you can. Find kinship with nature and preserve wild places and critters your whole life and share this enthusiasm "down trail" with whomever you cross paths with.

LEE STETSON AND HALF DOME

"WHAT STRUCK ME MOST ABOUT MUIR WAS HIS AMAZING ABILITY TO WRITE PASSIONATELY AND POETICALLY."
— LEE STETSON

The Battle over Hetch Hetchy

Over 90 percent of Yosemite's visitors make it to the famous Yosemite Valley. But a lesser-known and perhaps just as beautiful valley is Yosemite's Hetch Hetchy. Hetch Hetchy also has towering, dramatic cliffs and plunging waterfalls, and once it was a beautifully flowered and meadowed valley with a river meandering through it. But well over a century ago, San Francisco proposed to build a dam at the end of the valley to create a reservoir for the city's growing population. Beginning around 1901, John Muir and the Sierra Club led a campaign to preserve Hetch Hetchy Valley. It was a long battle, and eventually Muir and the conservationists lost. In 1913 Congress passed the Raker Act, which allowed the city of San Francisco to construct a dam and fill Hetch Hetchy Valley. In 1923 the O'Shaughnessy Dam was completed and the valley, as well as its natural and archaeological sites, was soon buried beneath the reservoir. For Muir the loss of this valley that he had fought for so passionately was a monumental defeat. Today many people feel a deep sadness that Hetch Hetchy Valley is gone, and there is a movement to restore this valley to its natural state. Many feel that a larger, more efficient dam can be created downstream, allowing for San Francisco's water supply as well as the return of a beautiful, natural valley to Yosemite. If you visit Hetch Hetchy now and stand on the dam, imagine how beautiful the valley was before the reservoir was created.

HETCH HETCHY BEFORE THE DAM

DAM HETCH HETCHY! AS WELL DAM FOR WATER-TANKS THE PEOPLE'S CATHEDRALS AND CHURCHES, FOR NO HOLIER TEMPLE HAS EVER BEEN CONSECRATED BY THE HEART OF MAN.

—JOHN MUIR

O'SHAUGHNESSY DAM AT HETCH HETCHY

HUMAN HISTORY IN YOSEMITE

8000 years ago: American Indians enter Yosemite Valley and occupy the area for thousands of years, calling it the "place of the gaping mouth."

1833: Explorers discover Yosemite Valley, encountering leaping waterfalls.

1848: Gold is found in the Sierra Nevada foothills. Miners flock to the region and disputes with American Indians begin.

1851: The Mariposa Battalion, in pursuit of Indians, finds the Yosemite Valley.

1855: James Hutchings leads the first tourists into Yosemite Valley.

1864: President Lincoln deeds Yosemite Valley and the Mariposa Grove to the state of California for protection.

1868: John Muir visits Yosemite for the first time. He will become a regular visitor to the area, and a move toward conservation begins.

1872: Yellowstone becomes the world's first national park.

1890: Yosemite becomes a national park by act of Congress. Areas deeded to the state of California in 1864 are not yet included.

8000 years ago   1833   1848   1851   1855   1864   1868   1872   189

1892: John Muir helps establish the Sierra Club and becomes the club's first president.

1903: Muir and President Theodore Roosevelt meet at Yosemite and camp at Glacier Point, discussing the need for federal protection of Yosemite.

1906: The Yosemite Valley and Mariposa Grove are transferred out of the state government's control and into Yosemite National Park.

1907: The Yosemite Valley Railroad begins taking visitors to El Portal to board stagecoaches for the rest of the journey into Yosemite.

1913: The Raker Act passes, calling for a dam in Hetch Hetchy Valley.

1916: The National Park Service is founded.

1923: O'Shaughnessy Dam is completed; the filling and drowning of Hetch Hetchy Valley begins.

1932: The Wawona area is added to Yosemite National Park.

1968: The Yosemite firefall tradition of dropping burning embers from Glacier Point into the valley ends.

1970: Free shuttle bus service starts in Yosemite Valley.

TODAY: You visit the park!

1892 1903 1906 1907 1913 1916 1923 1932 1970 Today

EARLY PARK HISTORY

Buffalo Soldiers

In the late 1800s and early 1900s, under the direction of Congress, African American soldiers patrolled some western national parks. They were America's original national park rangers, patrolling the parks before the National Park Service was created, in 1916. Yosemite and nearby Sequoia and Kings Canyon National Parks were part of this patrol.

GO SEE IT! Ranger Shelton Johnson performs his "Yosemite through the Eyes of a Buffalo Soldier" living history program throughout the summer in the Yosemite Theater. Check out the park newspaper, *Yosemite Guide*, for the latest performance schedule.

BUFFALO SOLDIERS FROM THE 24TH MOUNTED INFANTRY

Nicknamed the "Buffalo Soldiers," eight troops of the 9th Cavalry and a company of the 24th Infantry served this region, in 1899, 1903, and 1904. The soldiers evicted poachers, stopped people from taking timber illegally, and put out fires. One of their roles was to construct the first marked nature trail in the National Park System, which was set up near the Merced River. Their service is especially significant because it was at a time when much of the country was divided on whether whites and African Americans should get equal treatment.

One particular Buffalo Soldier stands out in history: Captain Charles Young, who was on patrol in Sequoia National Park in 1903 and became the acting military superintendent of Sequoia and General Grant National Parks (now Kings Canyon). He was the first African American to hold such a position. A sequoia in the Giant Forest in Sequoia National Park is named in Young's honor.

"THE BUFFALO SOLDIERS—AFRICAN AMERICAN MEN—WERE VITAL TO THE PROTECTION OF BOTH YOSEMITE AND SEQUOIA...AND THEY WERE AMONG THE FIRST PARK RANGERS."

—SHELTON JOHNSON

THE BUFFALO SOLDIERS

AN INTERVIEW WITH
YOSEMITE PARK RANGER
SHELTON JOHNSON

Q: WHERE HAVE YOU WORKED WITHIN THE NATIONAL PARK SYSTEM?

A: I began in Yellowstone in 1984 and was there for seven years. From there I went to the National Capitol Parks/East in Washington, DC, for a year and a half. Then my next position was at Great Basin— Nevada's only national park. One of the things I got to do there was lead cave tours inside Lehman Caves, where I would sometimes play the clarinet while guiding the tours. Finally, I have been here in Yosemite for the last seventeen years.

Q: WHAT IS YOUR POSITION AT YOSEMITE?

A: I am a park ranger in interpretation and education. One of the things I got to develop here was a program on the Buffalo Soldiers of the Sierra Nevada. It's a living history program where I portray a Buffalo Soldier as if it was 1903 to 1904. Wearing a 9th Cavalry uniform, I speak in a Southern dialect specific to a particular region of South Carolina. "Yosemite through the Eyes of a Buffalo Soldier" is the name of the program. It takes place in the Yosemite Theater. I've also led guided walks in the valley in costume and character while riding a horse, as that is how the Buffalo Soldiers got around while on patrol here at the park.

Q: WHAT DO YOU WISH VISITORS TO YOSEMITE AND ALL NATIONAL PARKS KNEW ABOUT THE BUFFALO SOLDIERS?

A: I want people to know that African Americans played an important role in America's national park history. There is evidence that African Americans don't visit national parks in great numbers—and certainly don't typically work in them as rangers, especially in wilderness areas like Yosemite. Well, the Buffalo Soldiers—African American men—were vital to the protection of both Yosemite and Sequoia before the creation of the National Park Service, and they were among the first park rangers. They built the first trail to the top of Mt. Whitney (in Sequoia National Park), which in those days was the highest mountain in the US, as well as building the first museum in what would become the National Park System, an arboretum, or display of trees and plants, in the southern section of Yosemite National Park. I wish people knew more about this.

Q: WHAT DID YOU TALK ABOUT WITH PRESIDENT OBAMA?

A: Several things, but one stands out. We both have seen bison up close in Yellowstone—me as a park ranger and President Obama as a visitor. So we swapped bison stories!

Q: ANY OTHER THOUGHTS?

A: I just want Americans to know that national parks are for everyone—people from every conceivable background, and that includes Yosemite. We get nearly four million visitors a year from all over the world. This is a place of exquisite beauty, and I hope everyone can enjoy it and continue to play a role in its protection!

PARK RANGER SHELTON JOHNSON IN YOSEMITE

RANGER SHELTON JOHNSON MEETS PRESIDENT OBAMA AT THE WHITE HOUSE

You can see Yosemite Park Ranger Shelton Johnson featured in the Ken Burns television series *National Parks: America's Best Idea*. Mr. Johnson was invited to the White House to preview the film with President Barack Obama in attendance.

Yosemite Cemetery

Around 1870 a cemetery was established in Yosemite Valley. You can see it by walking across the street from and just west of the Yosemite Museum. The American Indian people of Yosemite, for hundreds of years, buried their dead at the site of the current cemetery. There are marked graves within the cemetery and a guidebook on the history of the people buried there.

Pioneer History

In the Wawona area of the park, which is quieter and more rustic than Yosemite Valley, is the Pioneer History Center. There, you can walk through a covered bridge over the Merced River right into a nineteenth-century village. There are homesteads, a blacksmith shop, a cavalry office, a ranger patrol cabin, a bakery, a Wells Fargo office, and an old jail. The structures in the village are original buildings which were moved from different parts of Yosemite to Wawona. Stagecoach rides are also offered to visitors in Wawona, in coaches reminiscent of those that took visitors to the valley in 1875.

ART IN THE PARK

Ansel Adams

A number of artists have lived in the Yosemite area or make it their home today. Perhaps the park's most famous artist is Ansel Adams. When he first came to Yosemite at the age of fourteen, in 1916, his parents gave him a Box Brownie camera. He used it to explore the park and keep a visual journal. He came back to Yosemite in 1921 to be the curator of the LeConte Memorial Lodge, which was then the valley's visitor center. Adams led hikes and backpacking trips throughout the park. He spent lots of time taking pictures during these trips, but he also had other interests, such as being a concert pianist. Adams practiced piano at the studio of landscape painter Harry Best in the valley, getting to know Harry and his daughter, Virginia.

In 1927 Adams hiked to the shoulder of Half Dome, carrying a large view camera with him. He took pictures of the face of Half Dome, including one of his most famous photos. It was soon after this trip that Adams realized he wanted to focus his life on photography. He still, however, continued his visits to Best's Studio, and in 1928 he and Virginia were married there. In 1936 Harry Best died and left Adams and Virginia his studio (which is now the Ansel Adams Gallery). They stocked it

ANSEL ADAMS

with books, crafts, and photo supplies and also lived there, along with their children, for three decades. In the meantime Adams was hired to take photos of events all over the park. But he also took photos while out on his own, and these turned out to be some of his most prized works, used to promote the beauty of the natural world.

Adams focused his photography on the American West, especially Yosemite. His unique style involved determining just the right exposure and contrast needed to achieve the precise clarity and depth he sought in his photos. Later in life he and his wife moved to Carmel, California, and they passed down the studio to their son, Michael, and daughter-in-law, Jeanne Falk Adams, who renamed the studio the Ansel Adams Gallery. Adams died in 1984, but the gallery remains as the oldest family-run business in all of the National Park System.

"PHOTOGRAPHER ANSEL ADAMS HAS BEEN A **VISIONARY** IN HIS EFFORTS TO **PRESERVE** THIS COUNTRY'S WILD AND SCENIC AREAS...IT IS THROUGH HIS **FORESIGHT AND FORTITUDE** THAT SO MUCH OF AMERICA HAS BEEN **SAVED** FOR FUTURE AMERICANS."

—FORMER PRESIDENT JIMMY CARTER, 1980, ON AWARDING ANSEL ADAMS THE PRESIDENTIAL MEDAL OF FREEDOM

GO SEE IT! The Ansel Adams Gallery has been open for business in Yosemite Valley since 1902. You can find it right next to the Yosemite Valley Visitor Center. The gallery has unique crafts, books, and art, and a collection of Ansel Adams photos for sale.

CAPTURING YOSEMITE'S BEAUTY

AN INTERVIEW WITH STAFF PHOTOGRAPHER, ANSEL ADAMS GALLERY, AND YOSEMITE PARK RANGER

CHRISTINE LOBERG

Q: WHAT IS SPECIAL ABOUT TAKING PICTURES AT YOSEMITE?

A: The grandeur and the size of everything. It is just overwhelming, especially from a child's point of view. Everything here is huge and awesome in scale.

Q: HOW CAN KIDS LEARN MORE ABOUT PHOTOGRAPHY AT THE PARK?

A. One way is to take classes. One single-session class is offered at the gallery every Tuesday and Saturday all summer long, at 11 a.m. We take kids of all ages out into the park to learn about photography, and then practice. The only thing participants need to bring with them is a camera and a willingness to explore. Kids shoot up at trees, take pictures of tiny bugs, try looking at things and taking photos from various angles, anything that makes what they have in that lens look more interesting.

Q: WHAT ARE SOME TIPS FOR ASPIRING PHOTOGRAPHERS HERE AT YOSEMITE?

A: Take vertical and horizontal photographs. Compose the photo so that there is something in each section of the possible picture—like a grid. Get super close to the subject and take pictures from that angle.

CHRISTINE LOBERG

When taking pictures of grandeur, such as a giant sequoia or Yosemite Falls, make sure you have something in the foreground that can show how massive the main feature is—such as a person or rock to compare the tree or falls to. When taking close-ups—like tree bark or pine needles—look for little surprises, such as bugs or other objects within the photo. Don't only look for animals, but take pictures of places where animals have been and left signs behind. Burrows, bear claw marks, and holes in a tree from a bird also make for great photos!

Q: CAN YOU TELL US ANYTHING ELSE ABOUT TAKING PICTURES AT THE PARK?

A: We're in an amazing place. And one thing I think we can all think about is respecting Yosemite, and nature—so take only pictures, leave only footprints, and let nature be as it was when we first got here.

**"YOSEMITE FIRE AND MOON,"
BY CHRISTINE LOBERG**

MAYBE WE SHOULDN'T HAVE DONE THAT?

In the past, some things happened in Yosemite that wouldn't be allowed today. The sheep that John Muir despised were allowed to graze the meadows. A giant sequoia was cut out for cars to drive through. Bears were fed in open garbage pits while tourists came to watch. But perhaps Yosemite's most dramatic past event was the firefall...

The Famous Firefall

Every evening in Camp Curry a hushed crowd would gather until a man called out, "Let the fire fall!" Then, after a faint reply was heard from far above, a bonfire of red fir bark would be pushed over the edge of the cliff at Glacier Point, looking to those at Curry Village like a glowing waterfall of sparks and fire.

The iconic tradition began after James McCauley built a trail from the valley to Glacier Point, in 1871. He would sometimes build a fire near the cliff's edge at Glacier Point for guests at the Mountain Home Lodge. One night he pushed the fire over the edge. Those who saw this spectacle from the valley were amazed at the sight, and thus the firefall was born. Soon after, visitors could request the firefall for a fee of $1.50, and McCauley's twin sons would carry supplies up the trail to get the fire ready by dusk.

In 1899 David and Jenny Curry set up a camp below Glacier Point, calling it Camp Curry. To attract guests, the Currys made the firefall a nightly tradition. David Curry had a booming voice, and he would shout up to Glacier Point to the fire tender, "Is the fire ready?" The tender far above then replied, "The fire is ready!" Then Curry called out, "Let 'er go, Gallagher."

328. THE FIRE FALL, GLACIER POINT.

CAMP CURRY

POSTCARD FEATURING THE FIREFALL

**WOOD FOR THE FIREFALL
AT GLACIER POINT**

And the tender shoved the glowing embers off the cliff. This tradition continued off and on for decades, until 1968. Crowds would gather at Camp Curry long before dark for the 9 p.m. firefall drop. In later years the caller yelled up, "Hello, Glacier!" and the response was "Hello, Camp Curry!" Then the caller shouted, "Let the fire fall." The final reply was "The fire is falling!" The tender paid special attention to pushing the embers off the cliff evenly, to give the impression of a waterfall of fire.

THE FIREFALL

AN ACCOUNT FROM
PARK MUSICIAN AND HISTORIAN
TOM BOPP

I never got to see the firefall personally, so I feel like it is something I missed. Instead, I have collected old movies and soundtracks from the event and pieced together what the firefall was like. I now have a DVD and a show that combines music and actual clips of the firefall with some of the preparation as crews gather the bark. Then you can hear that creaking of the gate as it is opened to let the ball of fire drop. You can even make out the shouting from Camp Curry to Glacier Point, signaling it is time to drop the firefall. And we have also captured some of the murmured responses from the crowd. I guess seeing it on video, now, is the next best thing to being there....

**HISTORIC ENTRANCE
TO CAMP CURRY**

The firefall's last summer was 1967, when it was still being scheduled every night. There were some scheduled drops in autumn that year, too, and even a few in winter. There were several reasons why the event finally came to an end. First of all, by the 1960s, Yosemite had nearly two million visitors a year—many more than when the firefall first started. There were constant traffic jams of people trying to get to a good view of the firefall. And the meadows were being trampled over. Some of them were so impacted that they looked like badly kept-up footballs fields. There was even a streak on the cliff face where the fireball scorched the lichens on the rock. Also, it took about ten wheelbarrows full of bark each night to produce the firefall. Crews had to go farther and farther out to get the dwindling supply of bark—even driving all the way to Tioga Road! We know now that the removal of tree bark hurts the soil. This also affects the insect population, which in turn impacts the birds. Furthermore, Camp Curry put a good deal of time and labor into producing this free event. All these reasons led to the end of the firefall on January 25, 1968.

GO SEE IT! Tom, whose material includes the Firefall, has performed music and songs at the Wawona Hotel since 1983 and also appears at various other venues in the park.

TOM BOPP ENTERTAINING IN YOSEMITE

3 IT'S ALL ABOUT THE ROCKS

Perhaps the most outstanding of all Yosemite's features are its towering granite cliffs. These massive structures are easily seen from roads and viewpoints all over the park. There is no other place in the world with such sheer-walled granite scenery.

GEOLOGIC HISTORY

Creating an Amazing Valley

OVER 50 MILLION YEARS AGO the process that formed Yosemite's famous valley and all of the Sierra Nevada began. That's when deposits of silt, mud, and marine animal skeletons started accumulating on the ocean floor. Around 50 million years ago these deposits began uplifting into a mountain range. Molten rock rose beneath the mountains and hardened at their base. Rock formed by molten materials is called "igneous" rock. The coarsely grained igneous rock in Yosemite is granite.

ABOUT TEN MILLION YEARS AGO the whole range of mountains uplifted further and shifted west. This quickened the flow of the Merced River and its erosion formed a much deeper valley. Also around this time, the overall climate grew cooler.

ABOUT THREE MILLION YEARS AGO a canyon began forming in the region. The river raged through it, cutting a deeper and deeper chasm, up to three thousand feet deep. The weather cooled even more and the Ice Age began.

FROM ONE MILLION TO 250,000 YEARS AGO deep glaciers filled the canyon, all the way to the top. Huge sheets of ice cut into the Yosemite Valley, forming it into a U-shape with abrupt cliffs on its sides. The rock known today as Half Dome stuck out about 900 feet above the thick layer of ice. A vertical joint or fracture in Half Dome caused it to split and the glaciers carried away boulders and debris over time.

ABOUT 30,000 YEARS AGO a smaller glacier, known as Yosemite Glacier, protruded into the valley ending near Bridalveil Fall.

AROUND 10,000 YEARS AGO the last major glacier of Yosemite Valley finally melted, and it left behind a moraine, or pile of rocks, at its end which created a natural dam. This turned Yosemite Valley into a shallow lake. At its largest, Lake Yosemite was about five and a half miles long. Over time, it began to fill up with sediment—sand, gravel, and rocks carried by water—and the valley became a swampy meadow. The lake eventually filled completely. The ground leveled out and dried up, and the valley was as we see it today.

DID YOU KNOW?

As recently as around ten thousand years ago, Yosemite Valley was a lake! Once five and a half miles long, the lake eventually filled up with sediment and became the famous valley we know today.

The Great Debate

Today we have a clear sense of how Yosemite Valley was formed. But in the late 1800s a great debate occurred regarding the valley's origins. On one side was a trained geologist, Josiah Whitney. In 1863 he completed a geological survey of California. Whitney's observations led him to believe that Yosemite Valley was created by faulting, or large cracks, in the rocks that caused them to move. He thought that the valley was part of a large block that simply dropped down between two faults. Whitney did not believe that glaciers had anything to do with the valley's creation.

On the other side of the debate was John Muir. After arriving in the valley in 1868 and exploring for several years, Muir became convinced that glaciers had played a large role. In Alaska, Muir had seen firsthand the power of glaciers and how they shaped the land.

The dispute lasted for decades. Eventually the US government sent a team of geologists to the valley: in 1913 François Matthes and Frank Calkins began their long and thorough study of the area. Their observations led to this conclusion: Yosemite Valley had indeed been greatly modified or shaped by glaciers. Unfortunately, Muir did not live long enough to see his theory upheld in their report.

YOSEMITE'S SISTER PARK
IN CHINA, HUANGSHAN

YOSEMITE'S LONG-LOST SISTER

On the other side of the world, in eastern China, is a national park similar to Yosemite, Huangshan Park. Huangshan means "yellow mountain." On May 13, 2006, managers from both parks met and signed an agreement that the two "sisters" would form an alliance. The purpose of this effort is to work together and partner with organizations related to each park. And the two parks do have a lot in common! Both have granite cliffs, sculpted mountains, cascading waterfalls, and towering pines. Both also have a longstanding fascination for visitors, poets, painters, and photographers. Huangshan Park is also known for its hot springs, lush ferns, and Lotus Peaks—6,115 feet high, with sixty thousand stone steps leading to the summit. And there is one other thing both Yosemite and Huangshan have in common: they are World Heritage Sites. Yosemite made the list in 1984, and Huangshan was added to the list in 1990.

Domes, Domes, Domes

The many huge, bare, rounded granite formations in Yosemite are called domes. Some of the famous ones are Sentinel, Wawona, Lembert, Polly, Pothole, North Dome, Basket, and the world's most famous dome, Half Dome.

Domes are found all over the world, but they are especially common in the Sierra Nevada. Granite forms below the earth's surface, slowly cooling and crystallizing. This underground granite is under tremendous heat and pressure. During periods of mountain building, the granite is pushed up above the earth's surface. Then, slowly, the rock that overlays the granite erodes, and the pressure on the granite is reduced. Now the granite expands. Fractures, or joints, appear on its surface. Over time, the surface of the granite erodes in layers—like an onion—forming the rounded masses of rock we call exfoliation domes.

Not everyone can get to the top of Half Dome. But there is another great dome-hiking option in the park. Scrambling to the top of Lembert Dome, just north of Tuolumne Meadows, can be just as spectacular as summiting Half Dome. The two-mile Lembert Dome trail leads you to the base of the dome's back side. Then a series of scrambles up bare granite take you to the top. From there you get a 360-degree panorama of Yosemite's high country and all of Tuolumne Meadows. A small-scale version of Lembert, across the meadows to the west, is little Pothole Dome. The climb to the top of Pothole is about a 200-foot scramble. An added attraction of this rock adventure is that there are great examples of glacial polish along the way.

LEMBERT DOME

TENAYA LAKE AND POLLY DOME

A LONE JEFFREY PINE ON SENTINEL DOME

HIKERS ASCEND LEMBERT DOME

43

WHY ONLY HALF A DOME?

Half Dome is Yosemite's most famous rock and, some say, California's best-known natural feature. It rises 4,737 feet above the valley floor and is an impressive sight from any angle. Although it looks like it has been sliced in half, the dome never really was a fully rounded dome like North Dome. About 20 percent of Half Dome's other half was scoured away by glaciers. The rest of the shaping of Half Dome was done by erosion, as exposed surfaces cracked and peeled away over time. This is typical of all Sierra domes.

GO SEE IT!

A four-hour round-trip bus tour can take you 3,200 feet above the valley to Glacier Point. From there you can see all of the valley, Yosemite Falls, Vernal Fall and Nevada Fall, the high country, and an amazing straight-ahead view of Half Dome. This extremely popular ride leaves three times a day in summer from Yosemite Lodge. Tickets are available at Yosemite Lodge, the Curry Village check-in desk, and the tours desk in Curry Village. There are also one-way tickets for those who want to hike back down, either by the Panorama Trail or the Four Mile Trail.

ACTIVE FORCES

Rock Falls

Look out below! On October 8, 2008, seventeen thousand tons of granite (the equivalent of about 570 dump trucks full of rock) fell from the cliffs over Curry Village and onto the valley floor. The massive rock shower snapped trees, destroyed tents, and damaged cabins in this very popular part of the valley. The slide injured three people, but it could have turned out much worse.

Due to this rockfall and many others that have occurred in the area, the park permanently closed 233 tent cabins at Curry Village, as well as many buildings.

Rockfalls are nothing new to Yosemite Valley. In 1996 a much larger slide deposited more than eighty thousand tons of rock on the valley floor in the Happy Isles area. This slide killed one person and leveled many trees.

In March 1987, the largest rockfall in the history of Yosemite National Park pummeled the valley with about 1.5 million tons of rock at the base of Three Brothers, closing Northside Drive for several months.

But Curry Village seems to be the center of rockfall activity—since 1996, at least forty-six have hit in this area.

A ROCK SLIDE IN YOSEMITE VALLEY

CLIMATE CHANGE COMES TO YOSEMITE

AN INTERVIEW WITH OUTDOOR PHOTOGRAPHER AND NATURE WRITER

TIM PALMER

Q: WHAT SIGNS ARE THERE THAT YOSEMITE IS BEING AFFECTED BY GLOBAL WARMING?

A: Scientists agree that the melting of glaciers is the most visible sign of global warming worldwide. Here in Yosemite we have two glaciers—Lyell and Maclure. Lyell is the second-largest glacier left in the Sierra. Projections are that these two masses of ice will be gone, melted away, in just a lifetime or two. The coming generations will no longer see those gleaming white ice fields all summer long, and the water that the glaciers provide long after the rest of the snow has melted will also be gone. The glaciers are a symbol of other changes that will be felt in many ways. The snowpack will be reduced by up to 80 percent in the next century, with huge effects on California water supplies as well as fish and the other life in our rivers, the whole way to the sea. And other habitat changes are occurring, with effects on animals such as the pika. This tiny rabbitlike fellow needs cold areas to survive. Because mountaintops in Yosemite no longer get as cold as they used to, there may be no place left for the little pikas unless they can find ways to adapt. Whitebark pines are also vulnerable to disease and pests and other problems that the trees have avoided in their high and cold elevations, which are not going to be as cold as they were. We've got to protect nature so that wildlife can survive as well.

TIM PALMER

MACLURE GLACIER

WHAT IS A CLACIER?

A glacier is a large sheet of ice created over a long period when more snow falls in winter than melts in summer. Once the ice sheet gets thick enough—usually at around ninety to a hundred feet, it starts to slowly creep downhill under its own weight. That is when it becomes a glacier. As the glacier separates from the stationary snow, cracks appear, called bergschrunds, at the upper end of the glacier. Seeing these cracks helps geologists to know that an ice sheet is moving, and that it is a glacier rather than just a large patch of snow. If the ice sheet melts to the point where it no longer moves, it isn't a glacier anymore. Climate change is causing this to happen to glaciers all over the world, including the few small ones still left in the Sierra.

Signs of Glaciers

Today we can see evidence of glaciers throughout the park:

U-SHAPED VALLEYS: Yosemite Valley's floor is a classic U shape. Glaciers create this shape when they gouge out canyons, whereas river-carved valleys typically have a V shape.

HANGING VALLEYS: Hanging valleys can be seen in the park where side glaciers didn't drop all the way down to the main valley. This created U-shaped valleys above the main valley floor. Bridalveil Valley, above the falls, is a perfect example.

MORAINES: These ancient rock piles were pushed along by the power of the glaciers. Once a massive sheet of ice melted and retreated, the moraine would be left at the end point of the glacier and along the sides. Moraines helped form what once was Lake Yosemite, where the valley floor is now.

ERRATICS: The large boulders called erratics are in locations where only a glacier's slow, powerful movement could have deposited them. They are not to be confused with boulders on the valley floor brought down by rockfalls. The domes around Tuolumne Meadows, including Pothole Dome, are a good place to see erratics.

GLACIAL POLISH: Throughout the park, granite surfaces can be found that are smooth to the touch, as if they were polished. This is called glacial polish and is caused by the weight and force of a glacier slowly moving over the rock's surface. The rocks around Tuolumne Meadows are a great place to see glacial polish.

ERRATIC BOULDERS DEPOSITED AT OLMSTED POINT BY GLACIERS

Today's Living Glaciers!

The large Ice Age glaciers of the past are gone. But there are two remaining glaciers within Yosemite, Maclure and Lyell. Both of these small glaciers can be seen on backpacking trips in the park's high country. It is likely that these tiny glaciers (each about a quarter-mile) will be gone because of increased temperatures on Earth within a few decades. Lyell has retreated about 70 percent, losing nearly three-quarters of its size, since John Muir first saw it in 1871.

THE U SHAPE OF YOSEMITE VALLEY

GLACIAL POLISH IN TUOLUMNE MEADOWS

4 THE BIRTH OF A SPORT

It all started here! For many, the sport of rock climbing was "born" in Yosemite. Although this isn't entirely true, once you look at Yosemite's massive cliffs it is easy to see why the park has that reputation. And there is a great deal of climbing history here.

YOSEMITE CLIMBING HISTORY

Famous Climbs

1875: George Anderson, barefoot and using iron pegs, climbed Half Dome five years after the California Geological Survey said it was "unclimbable." Later visitors used the rope he set in place to ascend to the summit of the dome along the same route.

1957–1958: Warren Harding spent forty-seven days setting up a route along Yosemite's largest cliff. It took Harding and a changing team of climbers over a year and a half to complete the first El Capitan climb. It has been said that the National Park Service required the group to stop during the summer because of traffic jams caused by onlookers.

1989: Using special equipment, Mark Wellman, a paraplegic, ascended the Shield Route on El Capitan with his

MARK WELLMAN AND MIKE CORBETT SUMMITING HALF DOME

**A CLIMBER AT
THE SUMMIT**

climbing partner Mike Corbett. The media followed the climbers, making it worldwide news. Then in 1991, Wellman and Corbett scaled Half Dome in thirteen days, again making international news. These became the first ascents of these two massive rocks by a person who couldn't walk.

Camp 4

In the 1950s and 1960s, when the sport of rock climbing began in earnest, a great deal of the action took place right at Camp 4 in Yosemite Valley. Some of the best climbers of the world gathered here to camp, tell stories, share and sell equipment, and learn from each other's techniques, ideas, and routes. The campground is located near several large boulders where climbers can still be seen today trying out "bouldering" climbs. But the National Park Service and Camp 4's climbers haven't always seen eye to

The Yosemite Mountaineering School and Guide Service has been in operation since 1969. This is a great place to start, for you or anyone you know who is interested in climbing. Classes and private climbs are offered at all ability levels, starting from first-time ascents to multi-day guided climbs. Group classes are offered for people ten years old or over. Families with children under ten years of age can take private lessons.

eye. Conflict came to a head when massive floods hit the valley in the winter of 1997. In an effort to create park housing above floodwater levels, NPS proposed to build employee housing in the Camp 4 area. But the rock climbing community banded together to protect the campground, eventually getting it listed on the National Register of Historic Places.

CAMP 4 AND THE COLUMBIA BOULDER

From the late 1970s until the early 2000s, Camp 4 was known as Sunnyside Walk-in Campground, but since then it has been renamed Camp 4 in honor of its historic significance. Many rock climbers still camp there today.

GO SEE IT! The Columbia Boulder is the most famous climbable rock at Camp 4. It is easily recognized today by the white thunderbolt painted next to it. You might wander by and see if any climbers are practicing their bouldering techniques on this or other nearby rocks.

Big Names on Big Walls

JULES EICHORN: Eichorn completed over twenty-six first ascents in the Sierra, including Yosemite, between 1930 and 1952. He was one of the first Californians to practice climbing techniques taught in the Alps. He also spent years teaching mountaineering skills to rangers in Yosemite. Eichorn Pinnacle, at 10,940 feet near Tuolumne Meadows, is named after this climbing pioneer.

DAVID BROWER: In 1934 Brower, a mountaineer in the Sierra, surveyed climbing routes and kept records for the Sierra Club. Also in 1934, Brower climbed in the high country for ten weeks, bagging sixty-three peaks and thirty-two first ascents. After World War II, Brower managed annual Sierra Club high-country trips and became an avid conservationist, leading the fight to stop a dam from being built at Utah's Dinosaur National Monument. He became the leader of several outdoor and wilderness organizations, including the Sierra Club, Friends of the Earth, the League of Conservation Voters, and Earth Island Institute.

JOHN SALATHE: Salathe was a blacksmith in Switzerland before coming to the United States. He found that the traditional pitons used for climbing in the Alps were too soft, so in California he used steel similar to what Ford was using in car axles. These much stronger pitons, known as Lost Arrows, are still manufactured; this brand and others like it are still used by rock climbers today. In 1946 Salathe used them to scale the northwest face of Half Dome. In 1947 he followed that up by climbing the Lost Arrow Spire. He also was part of the first ascent of Sentinel Rock, in 1950.

ROYAL ROBBINS: Robbins was one of the pioneers of American rock climbing and he made many first ascents on the big walls of Yosemite, from 1957 through the 1960s. Robbins was in favor of "clean climbing," where climbers leave the rock undamaged after their ascent by using equipment that can be released from the rock, instead of devices that are permanently left in place. Robbins was also part of the early Camp 4 movement and later became known for founding the outdoor clothing company Royal Robbins.

WARREN HARDING: A colorful character, Harding said of one of his climbs of El Capitan, "As I hammered in the last bolt and staggered over the rim, it was not at all clear to me who was the conqueror and who was conquered. I do recall that El Cap seemed to be in much better condition than I was." Besides being the leader, in 1958, of the first team to ascend the Nose on El Capitan, he completed twenty-eight first ascents in the Sierra. Harding garnered the nickname "Batso" by frequently hanging out in Yosemite overnight, perched on one of the park walls. He invented the "bat tent" for shelter on Yosemite's big walls and also used "bat hooks" to latch onto very small pieces of granite. He called these devices "BAT" for Basically Absurd Technology.

LYNN HILL: Lynn Hill began climbing at age fourteen. In the 1980s she focused on climbs at Yosemite and was often seen hanging around Camp 4. Many of her climbing accomplishments have centered on the big walls at Yosemite. She was the first woman to make it up climbs rated as extremely difficult, 5.12+/5.13. In 1993 she became the first person to free climb the Nose on El Capitan. "Free climbing" means using only hands, feet, and body to get up the cliff; ropes are there only to protect against a fall. In 1994, at age thirty-three, Lynn Hill returned to climb the Nose in twenty-four hours, starting at 10 p.m. on September 19. She currently runs climbing camps throughout the US.

GO SEE IT! To enjoy this unique sport by watching climbers, one of the best places in the valley is Swan Slab. This popular climbing area is just west of the base of Lower Yosemite Fall Trail and across from the lodge. Many beginning climbers hone their skills here, and there are usually friends and family members hanging out and watching.

Yosemite's Mega-monolith: El Capitan

El Capitan rises 3,593 feet above the valley floor and has been called the largest granite monolith in the world! El Capitan has been climbed in a day, but most routes take three to four days or longer. The duration of the climb depends on the route taken, the experience of the climber, and weather conditions. Climbers must pack up, and out, all their equipment, including water—the single heaviest item—and their sleeping gear, which gets fixed into the rock at night. Occasionally, at night or early in the morning, you might see lights on the rock as climbers use flashlights while cooking or preparing for their day.

CLIMBERS ON EL CAPITAN

THERE ARE OVER 70 CLIMBING ROUTES ON EL CAPITAN

GO SEE IT!

For observing expert big-wall climbing, there is no better rock than El Capitan. Vehicle pullouts, such as the one at El Capitan Meadows, allow you to gaze up at brave souls slowly working their way up this massive monolith. In summer, climbers can also often be seen along Tioga Road and Pothole Dome, near Tenaya Lake and around Tuolumne Meadows.

LINGO, GEAR, AND RATING SYSTEMS

Climber Talk

If you hang around some of the many climbing areas in the park, you might hear climbers using their special lingo. Here are a few key words and what they mean:

Anchor: something that keeps an object—such as a climber—in place.

Belay: to use a rope, attached to a metal protection device or another person, to a secure a climber by catching his or her weight in a fall.

Bouldering: short climbs without any rope, typically with a spotter and crash pad underneath to reduce or eliminate injuries from falls.

Carabiner: a metal looping device with a sprung or screwed-in gate. This device connects to a rope and piton to protect climbers from falls.

Crux: the toughest part of a climb.

Free Solo: climbing without any equipment. Falls can be fatal.

Pitch: a single section of rock that is about 150 feet high, a common length of climbing ropes.

Piton: A metal spike driven into a crack in the rock that anchors a climber once a carabiner and rope are attached to it.

Protection: any piece of gear or equipment that climbers use to protect themselves from falls, such as gear placed into the rock and also within the climber's rope or lifeline.

Rope: climbers often call out "rope" before tossing their lifeline down the cliff to belay off the rock. This is a warning to others to look out for the rope on its way down.

Spotter: a person who braces or supports a bouldering climber.

Top Roping: setting up a one-pitch climb to go up and down repeatedly, trying out different routes and techniques.

Traditional Climbing: climbers place gear along the way to protect themselves from falls.

HARDWARE SORT-OUT IN CAMP 4, 1969

Ten Thousand Pieces of Gear

There is no doubt that climbing is a huge part of Yosemite's history. And probably no one would agree with this statement more than climbing veteran and guide Ken Yager. Yager over the years has scaled El Capitan more than fifty times. He has also gathered together over ten thousand pieces of climbing equipment, as well as an endless number of stories and pictures of the early days of climbing in Yosemite. One example of the gear is an old iron piton made from the legs of a stove. Other nuts and cams—pieces of protection meant for keeping climbers on the rock—are also part of the collection. Yager's goal, as well as the Yosemite Climbing Association's, is to open up a climbing museum at the park. Yager can't wait for the museum to become a reality. As he says, "It is long overdue."

THE NAME GAME

Climbing routes often have colorful names. First ascenders give a route its name, and in many cases it sticks. There are many routes to climb El Capitan and Half Dome. Here are some of their names:

HALF DOME ROUTES	EL CAPITAN ROUTES
Snake Dip	Tangerine Trip
The Autobahn	Never Never Land
Big Chill	Horse Chute
Call of the Wild	Lost World
The Fast Lane	Squeeze Play
Happy Gully	Jolly Roger
Lost Again	Grape Race
Dome Polisher	Scorched Earth
Final Exam	Bad to the Bone
Solitary Confinement	Surgeon General
Queen of Spades	Lost in America
Gravity's Rainbow	

CLIMBING SCALE

1. *Walking with little risk of injury.*

2. *Steeper scrambling, with exposure and falls that could result in injuries.*

3. *Even steeper scrambling, with potential for serious injuries as a result of a fall.*

4. *Steep sections that could use rope. Unroped falls could lead to death.*

5. *True rock climbing on vertical or near vertical rock. Unroped falls lead to serious injury or death.*

How Hard Is That Climb?

The system now used worldwide to rate a climb's difficulty originated in Yosemite. Each route is graded, and the grades are based on opinions of climbers who have used it.

The Yosemite Decimal System has grades within five classes. Class five climbs start with 5.1 and go up to 5.15b, the latter being the hardest climbs in the world. Class five climbs are rated based on the crux, or hardest move, on the climb. Many climbs in the Yosemite area are rated between 5.3/5.4 and 5.11/5.12.

The Nose route on El Capitan, first climbed by Warren Harding in 1957 to 1958, has 31 pitches, or sections where the climbing rope is reset and secured, and is rated an extremely difficult 5.13.

"START EASY AND WORK YOUR WAY UP FROM THERE."
— ELIZA AMSTUTZ

STARTING AT THE TOP

AN INTERVIEW WITH YOUNG YOSEMITE CLIMBER ELIZA AMSTUTZ

Q: WHEN DID YOU START CLIMBING?

A: I started climbing when I was four or five years old, with top roping, which is when you secure a rope at the top of one rock so you can climb it over and over. This was at Swan Slab and Grant's Crack, in the valley. That's a good place for beginners. My first multi-pitch climb, when you resecure your rope over and over as you scale a large cliff, was when I was seven or eight, on the Manure Pile Buttress, also known as Ranger Rock. After those climbs I wanted to go again and again, especially multi-pitch climbs!

CARABINER

Q: WHAT ARE YOUR FAVORITE YOSEMITE CLIMBS?

ELIZA AMSTUTZ

A: I love the climbs around Tuolumne Meadows, such as Puppy Dome and Daff Dome. They are mostly one-pitch top ropes and a lot of fun. But last year I also climbed Cathedral Peak. That was about five to seven pitches and with amazing views from the top! I also just climbed one in the valley called Higher Cathedral Spire. We were so high off the ground I was a little freaked out. But when we got to the top it was totally worth it. I'd go back and do it again if I could.

Q: WHERE ELSE HAVE YOU CLIMBED AND WHAT IS SPECIAL ABOUT CLIMBING IN YOSEMITE?

A: In winter and spring my family also takes me to Joshua Tree, in the desert, to climb. But what is neat about Yosemite is the amazing views you get from the tops of the climbs. Also, there are a variety of rock surfaces, with cracks, faces, chimneys, and even glacial polish on climbs, making it all very interesting and challenging.

AT THE TOP

Q: WHAT SHOULD YOUNG CLIMBERS DO TO MAKE SURE THEY ARE SAFE?

A: They should make sure they have the right gear, and go with their parents or friends. If they don't know anyone who is an experienced climber, they could sign up for a class or a guided climb. They should bring their parents along, so they can learn too. If they learn how to belay, then you can all go climbing together. I usually climb with my dad, and we sometimes teach other friends too. Some of my best friends' parents are great climbers, and also work as guides, so I guess I'm pretty lucky to live here!

Q: WHAT ADVICE DO YOU HAVE FOR YOUNG PEOPLE LEARNING TO CLIMB?

A: Start easy and work your way up from there. Try to have fun and not get too upset if you don't make it to the top. You can always come down and try it again! Also, don't be scared of lowering. That's one of the funnest parts, but it's also really necessary. Lowering is the way you get down from top roping. Then later you can learn how to rappel by yourself. My little sister is so little and light it takes a long time to get down! Sometimes my dad has to even climb up and pull her down.

> **"WHAT IS NEAT ABOUT YOSEMITE IS THE AMAZING VIEWS YOU GET FROM THE TOPS OF THE CLIMBS."**
>
> — **ELIZA AMSTUTZ**

5 PLANTS! FROM MASSIVE TO MICROSCOPIC

From lower elevation scrub, grasses, and gray pine to deep forests and high-elevation wildflowers, Yosemite has many kinds of plants. It has nearly fifteen hundred types of plants that bloom! Because so many parts of Yosemite are at different elevations, blooms can be found in the park during much of the year. But the park is probably most famous for its giant trees.

SEQUOIAS: THE WORLD'S LARGEST LIVING THINGS

Life of a Sequoia

Sequoia trees and their relatives, the redwoods, are the largest living things on the planet. Sequoias only live naturally in California; redwoods mostly live along the coast of California and southern Oregon. The redwoods are famous for their height—some over 370 feet tall—but considering total volume of wood, the sequoia is the world's largest tree. One sequoia can weigh as much as forty-six fully grown male elephants, much more

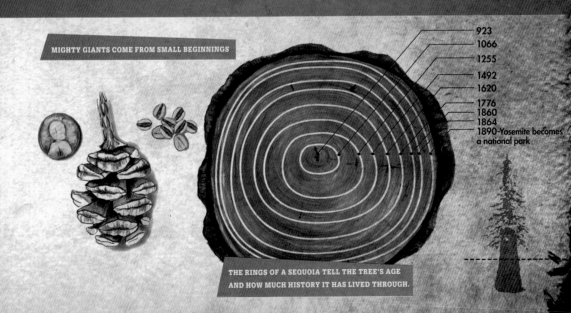

MIGHTY GIANTS COME FROM SMALL BEGINNINGS

923
1066
1255
1492
1620
1776
1860
1864
1890-Yosemite becomes a national park

THE RINGS OF A SEQUOIA TELL THE TREE'S AGE AND HOW MUCH HISTORY IT HAS LIVED THROUGH.

than a redwood. Giant sequoias can get as tall as 310 feet. The tallest in Yosemite is the Columbia Tree in the Mariposa Grove, at about 290 feet. Once sequoias are around two thousand years old, they are near their full height, but the trees continue to grow wider as they age.

Sequoia trees normally live well over two thousand years. They survive many droughts and fires, and human events as well. The inside of a sequoia can tell us how old the tree is. There is a series of circular rings working their way out from the middle, and each ring represents one year's growth. Scientists who use these rings to date the trees are called dendrochronologists. The width or thickness of a ring is determined by the growing conditions that year. If there was abundant rain and snow, a thick ring developed. A thin ring could indicate a drought. There even could have been a fire that stunted the growth of the tree that year. The fire-resistant bark of sequoias, up to three feet thick, helps them to survive fires. Some sequoias have fire scars that can be dated back three thousand years.

For new sequoias to grow, there must be fire. Fires heat up cones, causing them to open up and drop fresh seeds to the ground. Fires also clear space by burning pine and fir trees that crowd the forest. The cleared areas give the massive sequoia trees the sunlight they need to grow. Fires also enhance minerals in the soil that, when added to the moisture in the ground, make for perfect growing conditions for the trees. Giant sequoias produce thousands of cones in their lifetimes. Each cone has approximately two hundred seeds that are a quarter of an inch long, or about as big as an oat flake—and these tiny seeds become the world's largest trees!

GO SEE IT! There is a slice of a sequoia tree in front of the Yosemite Museum in the valley. The tree's rings are clearly evident, and some of the most visible ones are dated and connected to major world events.

SEQUOIA TREES NORMALLY LIVE WELL OVER TWO THOUSAND YEARS.

Discovering Giants

"Found some trees of the redwood species, incredibly large," wrote one of the explorers crossing the Sierra with Joseph "Snowshoe" Walker in 1833, but the printing shop that was to publish his report burned to the ground. Then, in 1852, A. T. Dowd found the Calaveras Big Trees while tracking a grizzly bear. His find was described in the *Sonora Herald,* and this was probably the first published record of the giant sequoias. From then on, many people journeyed to see them. One particular sequoia in the Calaveras groves, called the Father of the Forest, was reported to be measured at 450 feet long as it lay on the ground. Some reports said living sequoia trees were up to 600 feet tall and that if left alone they would grow to 1,000 feet. These stories were met with doubt and wonder. One of the Calaveras trees was chosen for display at the Crystal Palace exhibits in England and New York in 1855. The bark of the Mother of the Forest, as it was called, was stripped to 120 feet above the ground and, in order to save money, just the bark was shipped. The tree stayed alive, but only for a short time. John Muir despised this skinning of trees. He said it was "as sensible a scheme as skinning our great men would be to prove their greatness."

THE FAMOUS BOOLE TREE

In 1876 a sequoia was cut from the Grant Grove in what is now known as Sequoia and Kings Canyon National Park for the Philadelphia Centennial Exhibition, and the Mark Twain Tree, also in Kings Canyon, was chopped down in 1891 for display in a museum. In 1892 a third tree from this region, the General Noble Tree, was cut down, sawed into cross sections, and hauled to the World's Fair in Chicago for display. Even then some people debated the authenticity of a tree this size. They thought it was a fake.

Cutting Them Down

It was around the 1890s that commercial logging of sequoias began. But cutting them down was extremely difficult. One logger reported that a sequoia fell with such force that "mud and stones were driven near 100 feet high and they left their mark on nearby trees."

Up to three thousand fence posts could be made from a single tree, or 650,000 wood shingles, which is enough for seventy-five roofs. Soon several sequoia groves in the southern Sierra were stripped completely. In the Converse Basin grove in today's Giant Sequoia National Monument, fifty-three huge sequoias were cut down, but one giant, the Boole Tree, was saved. This tree, with its thirty-five-foot diameter, was preserved by Frank A. Boole, who was in charge of the Converse Basin logging. At 269 feet high and with a 113-foot circumference, the Boole Tree is the eighth-largest tree in existence. It stands alone among the much smaller, new-growth trees in the eerily harvested scene. Other areas, such as Stump Meadow in the Giant Sequoia National Monument, were completely stripped: one hundred sequoia stumps are visible in Stump Meadow.

STUMP MEADOW

WAWONA
26' THROUGH THE OPENING
CUT IN 1880

CIVILIAN CONSERVATION CORPS
WORKERS AT THE WAWONA TREE

A TUNNEL THROUGH A TREE?

National Park Service policies have changed over time. In some cases, promoting tourist attractions used to take priority over protecting natural features. A perfect example of this is in Yosemite's Mariposa Grove: the Wawona Tree, which was carved into a tunnel in 1881. The tree quickly became a hugely popular tourist attraction. Many people went to have their pictures taken in it, or to drive their coaches or cars through. The massive tree withstood the damage for almost ninety years. But the Wawona Tree could not take the winter of 1969. With about two tons of snow on its upper branches, the much-weakened tree collapsed that winter, after having lived for about twenty-two hundred years. Experts determined the causes of its death to be heavy snow, wet soil, and the tunnel.

In 1937 a giant sequoia fell in the Crescent Meadow area of Sequoia National Park. The next summer a tunnel was carved through the tree as an attraction. Today the National Park Service philosophy is to allow all features of the natural landscape, including downed trees, to evolve on their own without human intrusion. The National Park Service would not allow tunnels to be cut in giant sequoias today.

GALEN CLARK'S FUNERAL IN YOSEMITE

Save the Trees!

Despite all the enthusiasm for cutting and logging, a movement to protect the sequoias began. In 1864 the Mariposa Grove in Yosemite was granted to the state of California for preservation. Further efforts led to the creation of Sequoia National Park in 1890, with Yosemite shortly following. And much more recently, on April 15, 2000, President Bill Clinton designated thirty-three of the remaining sequoia groves not already protected in national or state parks as the Giant Sequoia National Monument. Perhaps after visiting the sequoias in Yosemite you'll be inspired to see more of these massive trees.

Galen Clark: Champion of the Trees

In 1848, after the death of his young wife, Clark came to California seeking gold. Within five years, he became severely sick with tuberculosis. Doctors said he had six months to live, and, as there was no other treatment, they recommended rest and fresh, outdoor air. Clark moved to Wawona to be a homesteader and "take my chances of dying or growing better, which I thought were about even."

In 1857 he became the first non-Indian to see Yosemite's Mariposa Grove of big trees. He spent much of the rest of his life exploring the grove and teaching others about the giant trees. Clark also became an advocate of protecting the grove, writing many letters to Congress and influential friends. This led to the Yosemite Grant being signed into law by President Lincoln in 1864, during the Civil War.

Clark's lungs healed and he explored, climbed, and led visitors throughout the area. He ran a small hotel and guide service and eventually wrote three books about Yosemite while also being the guardian of the Mariposa Grove for twenty-four years. He died in Oakland, California, in 1910, but he had chosen his burial site in Yosemite a few days before his ninety-sixth birthday. Clark dug his own grave and planted sequoia seedlings around it from the Mariposa Grove while also picking out a granite marker.

GO SEE IT! Today you can see Galen Clark's gravesite in the Yosemite Valley cemetery, as well as the maturing sequoia trees circling it. If you visit Clark's gravesite, you might take some time to appreciate how important he and other early naturalists were to Yosemite and think about how the park might look if they hadn't been here.

Where Can I Find Giants?

The giant sequoias living today can be traced back to the days of the dinosaurs and once grew all over the Northern Hemisphere. At least twelve fossil types of similar trees have been discovered in northern Europe, Iceland, Greenland, and Alaska. Also according to fossil evidence, giant sequoias lived in today's southern Idaho and western Nevada about ten to twenty million years ago, before the rise of the Sierra Nevada. Eventually the tree's range became restricted to the Sierra Nevada due to climate change; the seeds of these massive trees cannot sprout in hot, dry regions. But the sequoia still has living relatives elsewhere. The coast redwood of central and northern California and southern Oregon is a very similar tree. The bald cypress of the southern United States is another living relative. So are the dawn redwood of China and the summit cedar of Tasmania.

There are many famous sequoia groves in California. In addition to those found in Yosemite, sequoias can also be seen at Giant Sequoia National Monument and in Calaveras Big Trees State Park and Sequoia and Kings Canyon National Park, which is where the famous General Grant Tree grows. This tree is also known as "the nation's Christmas tree" and is the third-largest sequoia in existence.

DID YOU KNOW?

There are currently about seventy-five groves of giant sequoias in the world. All are in the central or southern Sierra Nevada of California. Sequoias thrive in cool moist climates with plenty of winter snow, water from melting snow in the spring, and summers that are pleasant and not too warm. Elevations for the groves range between 4,500 and 7,500 feet.

GALEN CLARK (CENTER, WITH LITTLE GIRL) AND FRIENDS AT THE WAWONA TREE

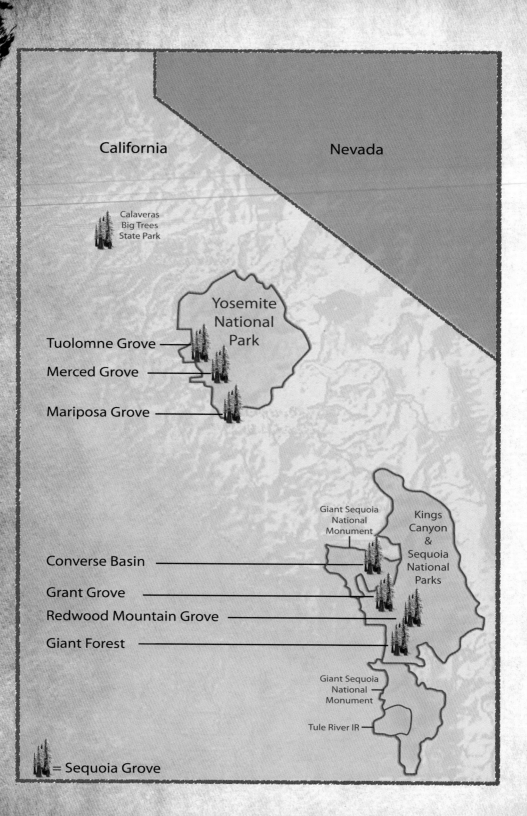

California

Nevada

Calaveras
Big Trees
State Park

Yosemite
National
Park

Tuolomne Grove

Merced Grove

Mariposa Grove

Giant Sequoia
National
Monument

Kings
Canyon
&
Sequoia
National
Parks

Converse Basin

Grant Grove

Redwood Mountain Grove

Giant Forest

Giant Sequoia
National
Monument

Tule River IR

= Sequoia Grove

THE GRIZZLY GIANT

Yosemite's most famous sequoia is the Grizzly Giant. This massive tree is 209 feet tall, the twenty-fifth-largest sequoia in existence. The two-thousand-year-old tree is right along a popular trail in the Mariposa Grove. But the Grizzly Giant is actually the second-largest tree in the grove, as the Washington Tree is slightly larger. The General Sherman Tree in Sequoia National Park, about one hundred miles south of Yosemite, is believed to be between twenty-three hundred and twenty-seven hundred years old. It is one of the tallest giant sequoia trees in the world, with a height of about 275 feet. This tree is known as the world's biggest tree in terms of volume. As of 2002, its trunk measured about 52,513 cubic feet.

GO SEE IT!

Check out this museum for trees. In the heart of the Mariposa Grove, about two miles from the parking area, is the Mariposa Grove Museum. You'll want to head up there on foot or a tram tour, because some of the best sequoias surround it. The museum, originally built in 1930, is on the site where Galen Clark first constructed a cabin, in 1861, while he was a guardian of the grove. Now the building is on the National Register of Historic Places and features exhibits and information on sequoias as well as a gift shop.

THE BACHELOR AND THREE GRACES IN MARIPOSA GROVE

Sequoia Groves in Yosemite

MARIPOSA GROVE: The Mariposa Grove is at the south end of the park, near Wawona. This is Yosemite's largest and most visited grove. There are at least six hundred very large sequoias here and hundreds of smaller, younger ones. The most famous tree in the Mariposa Grove is the massive Grizzly Giant. The Washington Tree in the upper part of the grove is even larger than the Grizzly Giant and it is the largest sequoia north of the Kings River. The famous Wawona Tunnel Tree, once known as the "most photographed tree in the world," is here. Other famous trees in the grove are the Telescope Tree (where you can stand inside and look right up through it to the sky) and the Clothespin Tree (you'll see how it got its name when you get there). Access to the grove is made easy by free buses running all day long from the Wawona area in summer.

TUOLUMNE GROVE: The Tuolumne Grove is off of Tioga Road near the junction with Big Oak Flat Road. A former road that runs through the grove is now used to make the very steep hike in to the big trees, about one mile. There are about fifteen large sequoias in the grove and many smaller ones. The Siamese Twins are two sequoias fused together at their base. The fallen tunnel tree might be the most interesting tree in the grove. Imagine what it was like standing! The King of the Forest is the largest tree in the grove, with a base circumference of 103 feet.

MERCED GROVE: The Merced Grove is off of Big Oak Flat Road on the western side of the park and is accessed by an easy trail. There are about fifteen large trees within the grove and many younger sequoias.

BIGGEST! TALLEST! OLDEST!

California has the world's tallest trees, redwoods; the world's largest trees in bulk, sequoias; and the world's oldest trees, bristlecone pines. Bristlecones grow just below treeline on some mountains of the western United States. They are the world's oldest single living organisms. And the oldest bristlecone, called Methuselah, is in the White Mountains of California, not far east of Yosemite. It is estimated to be nearly five thousand years old!

■ = Giant Sequoia

■ = Bristlecone Pine

■ = Redwood

MORE TREES

BLACK OAK: One very important tree in Yosemite is the black oak. These large trees live in lower elevations, such as Yosemite Valley. Black oaks are a vital food source for animals, including bears, deer, woodpeckers, and squirrels. Black oak acorns were once a staple of the local American Indian diet.

Aerial photos show that there are fewer trees now than fifty or sixty years ago, and scientists aren't certain why. One idea is that fire suppression policies of the past prevented oaks from dominating the forest as they once did. Another theory is that American Indians used to cultivate the forest through the use of fire, and they also protected young oak saplings. This created more extensive open oak woodland, but fewer large trees. An increase in the park's deer population is also thought to have reduced the number of oaks, as deer forage on small saplings.

DOGWOOD: The dogwood is another showy park tree. It grows in Yosemite forests and blooms from April until July, depending on the elevation. Dogwoods have distinctive white flowers that decorate the lower part, or understory, of the forest when in bloom.

DOGWOOD BRANCHES OVER THE MERCED RIVER

A BLACK OAK IN YOSEMITE VALLEY

Incense cedar

Jeffrey pine

Lodgepole pine

Mountain hemlock

Ponderosa pine

Red fir

Sequoia

Douglas fir

White fir

Sugar pine

DID YOU KNOW?

"Hyperion" is the name of a coast redwood tree in northern California that measures 379.1 feet high, ranking it as the world's tallest known living tree.

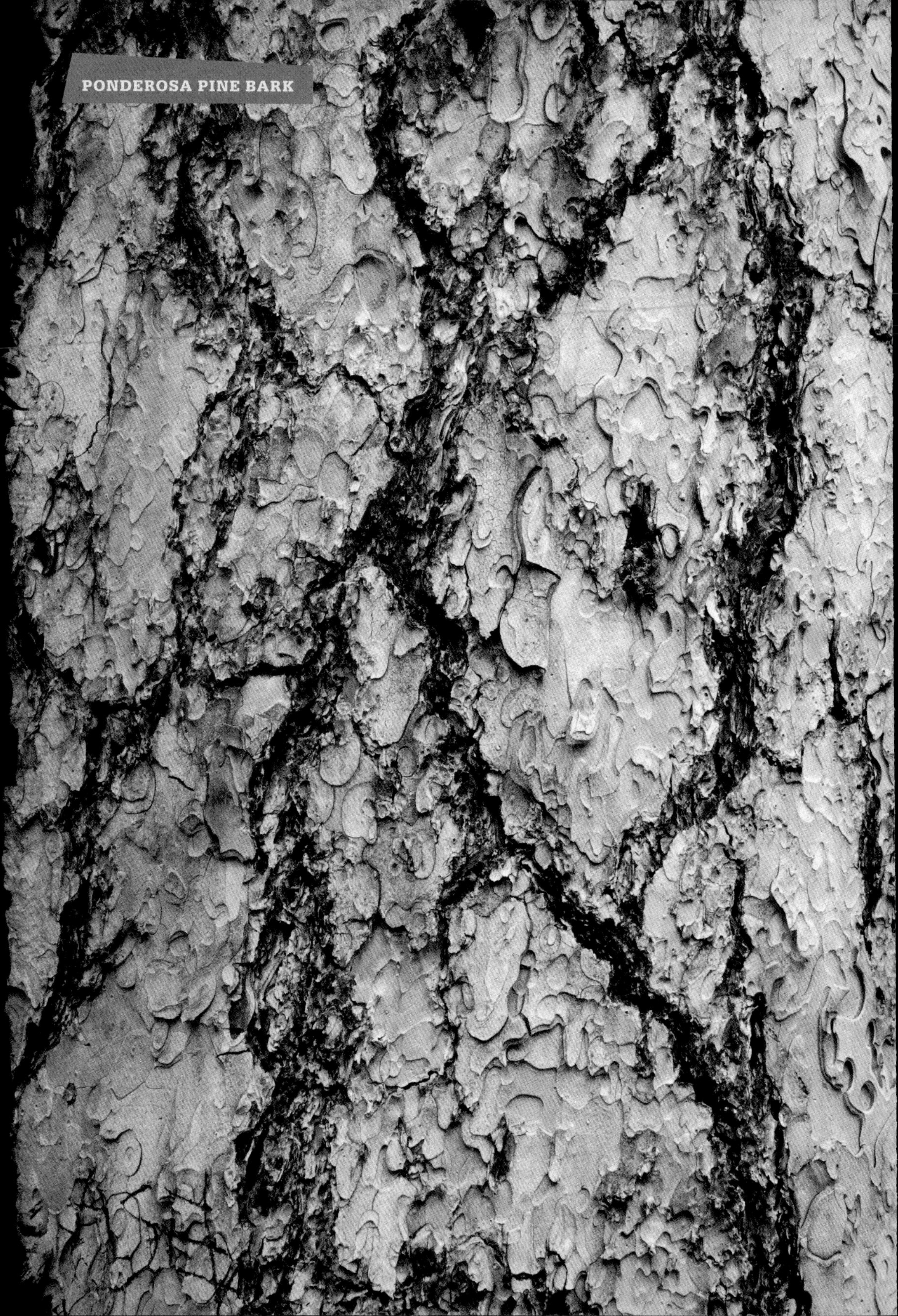

PONDEROSA PINE BARK

IS IT BUTTERSCOTCH OR VANILLA?

One of the most abundant trees in Yosemite Park is the ponderosa pine. These trees can be identified by smelling their bark, which has a vanilla or butterscotch aroma, although some say cinnamon or even coconut! The scent seems strongest between cracks in the bark and on warm summer days. Jeffrey pines, a close relative of the ponderosa, also give off that sweet scent. Check it out when you are hiking along a trail in the park.

Fall in Yosemite

As temperatures cool and the days get shorter, leaves on trees stop making chlorophyll, the chemical that makes them green. When this happens, Yosemite's fall colors are revealed. Aspen leaves turn vivid yellow, and oaks and cottonwoods also display their yellow leaves. Maples glow red and yellow. Dogwood leaves become a bright red—and so do poison oak leaves. The best conditions for fall colors are dry weather and temperatures just above freezing. Usually this is in late October in Yosemite, but it also depends on the elevation. Fall colors come to Yosemite Valley later than Glacier Point, which is much higher up.

BEAUTIFUL FALL COLORS IN YOSEMITE

WHAT'S THAT GROWING ON THE TREES?

Lichens—tiny, slow-growing, plantlike organisms made of fungi plus algae or bacteria—grow in abundance in Yosemite. Studies show that there could be at least five hundred species of lichens in the park. You can see them on trees and shrubs at lower elevations and clinging to rocks in the highest parts of the park. Some areas with year-round moisture, such as streaks along cliffs near waterfalls, can get coated black from lichen. Lichen populations are being carefully watched because their health often is a good indication of the health of the environment they live in. Air pollution, for example, affects lichen populations.

LICHEN GROWING ON A TREE

FIRES CAN BE GOOD FOR THE FOREST?

AN INTERVIEW WITH YOSEMITE NATIONAL PARK FIRE ECOLOGIST

GUS SMITH

Q: WHY ARE SOME FIRES GOOD?

A: Well, for starters, hot dry summers are the norm here, and historically the forests have always had fires—every five to ten years or so. But we'd been suppressing or controlling forest fires for fifty years until we changed our policy thirty years ago. Fire suppression leads to overgrown forests with lots of small trees. This doesn't allow larger trees to thrive, and larger trees are more fire resistant. But more importantly, overgrown forests are much more vulnerable to a massive, out-of-control fire. Forests with regular burns have natural fire scars or past burn areas that determine how far future fires can go. The forests don't get such hot fires, either, with so much of the overgrowth naturally eliminated.

Q: HOW DO YOU MONITOR FIRE DANGER LEVELS?

A: We keep track of historical drought indexes or patterns. For example, until the 2009-10 rain and snow season, we had been in a seven-year drought. Below-average precipitation raises the danger level for fires. Also, fuel moisture is monitored regularly from small, downed limbs and cut limbs, branches and litter. Dry wood is much more susceptible to lightning or other sources of ignition. In addition, the current weather plays a huge part. When it is hot, windy, and dry, with low humidity, and it has been a long time since it has rained, and the trees are stressed due to a prolonged drought, there is extreme fire danger.

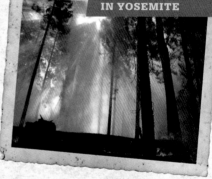

A CONTROLLED BURN IN YOSEMITE

YOSEMITE PARK RANGER GUS SMITH MEASURES A SEQUOIA

Q: WHAT HISTORICAL FIRES COME TO MIND THAT HAVE BEEN DEVASTATING?

A: The 1990 Arch Rock fire, which burned around eighteen thousand acres, and the Steamboat fire, which burned an additional eight thousand acres, were the most destructive in covering a significant part of the park and into the town of Foresta, burning many structures.

Q: WHY DO YOU HAVE CONTROLLED BURNS?

A: We prescribe burns and are allowed to cut trees up to twenty inches in diameter to keep the lower ladder of the forest clear. This allows for forests to thrive. But it also helps wildfires to be much more easily managed and less intense. They behave more predictably when the area has been receiving burns every five to ten years. If a part of the forest has not had a recent burn, ground litter piles up, making the area much more fire dangerous. We can only have a controlled burn, though, under certain weather conditions—winds must be very light, temperatures not too hot, and the humidity up. Prescribed burns guide the forests back into their natural state and they are more resilient to massive fires under this normal pattern.

Q: WHAT IF THERE IS A NATURAL FIRE—DO YOU PUT IT OUT?

A: We think every fire could be a good fire for the forest. And in 85 percent of the park's forests we can manage them this way—structures or roads are not threatened in the backcountry. But in 15 percent of the park, too many people and communities could be affected. We must put those fires out immediately. Backcountry fires, though, if they are in an area that has had regular burns, have natural fire breaks—old fire scars—and they are well-behaved. They only spread so fast and so far.

Q: WHEN ARE THE TIMES WHEN ALL CAMPFIRES OR FIRES OF ANY SORT ARE NOT ALLOWED?

A: Extreme fire danger is when moisture levels in wood are dangerously low and so is the humidity in the air. During these conditions, the probability of ignition—from any ash or cigarette or blowing ember—is incredibly high and therefore we stop all fires from being used or enjoyed within the park.

WILDFLOWERS

During spring in the lower elevations, orange California poppies dot the hills as well as lupine, monkeyflower, owl's-clover, and shooting stars, among others. Some good places to see early-season wildflowers are Cook's Meadow, Wawona Meadow, and the Wapama Falls trail out of Hetch Hetchy.

In the higher elevations, above 7,000 feet, spring comes much later. One very unusual blooming plant in this region is the snowplant. Up to one foot high, snowplant is a bright red color when it pops out from the last remaining thin layers of snow. Also in this region are mariposa lily, Yosemite aster, columbine, and red Indian paintbrush. The McGurk Meadow, Taft Point, and Sentinel Dome trails are nice places to see higher-elevation flowers in bloom.

Summer, too, in the high meadows is a time of abundant flowers. Streamside flowers include elephant heads, broad-leaved lupine, red heather, fireweed, great red Indian paintbrush, mountain monkeyflower, and waterplantain buttercup, among many more.

The Sierra's largest meadows are found right along Tioga Road near the eastern edge of the park, at Tuolumne Meadows. This area opens only when the highway is cleared of snow, usually by June. It is worth the wait, however, as the meadows that greet you in summer are beautifully carpeted in grass and wildflowers with clear cold streams running through, and surrounded by granite domes and high mountains that are often snowcapped much of the year.

Rocky, high-elevation areas have white heather, western wallflower, Sierra penstemon, red mountain heather, pussypaws, woolly sunflower, and many other wildflowers.

SPRING WILDFLOWERS IN YOSEMITE

GO SEE IT! The Soda Springs trail and the trail to Elizabeth Lake at Tuolumne Meadows are great places to see higher-elevation wildflower displays, as is the area around the base of Lembert Dome. There are also guided ranger walks in the Tuolumne area to help you identify the flowers.

Lupine

California poppy

Monkeyflower

Mariposa lily

Snowplant

Owl's-clover

Yosemite aster

Elephant heads

Pussypaws

Baby blue eyes

POISONOUS AND PESKY

Leaves of Three, Let It Be!

Poison oak grows all over the valley, especially farther west, toward the foothills. It is also common in the Hetch Hetchy area. Poison oak is easily identified in spring and summer by the distinctive ribbed pattern on its three leaves ("leaves of three, let it be"). The leaves are shiny green to reddish in color. But in winter, identifying poison oak can be tricky. The plant loses its leaves but still has living branches and stems that are hard to pick out. When a hiker accidentally touches any part of the plant and the oil or resin gets onto the skin, it may cause a mild to severe rash with blisters and incessant itching that can last for days. Watch for poison oak growing near the trail, especially in spring, when some plants overgrow the pathway.

Invasion of the Unwanted Plants

Over the years several non-native plants have found their way into Yosemite. These intruders affect wildlife, change fire zones, and alter the scenery. Park staff are trying different ways to remove these plants without harming the native flora. Removal techniques include hand pulling, lopping, and the use of herbicides and fire, and introducing bugs or plants that will destroy the invaders. Beetles, for example, will eat the seeds of certain plants. Several key invasive plants are being focused on. One that you might have seen without knowing it was invasive is velvet grass, which turns some of the park's meadows a light brown color rather than their typical green.

POISON OAK IS OFTEN FOUND WITH MANZANITA AND BABY OAKS.

POISON OAK AREA

6 THE WORLD'S SMARTEST BEARS AND OTHER FASCINATING WILDLIFE

From tiny salamanders and frogs to rare birds, such as the sooty grouse or black-backed woodpecker, to bears and other large mammals, wild creatures live throughout Yosemite.

SPECIAL STATUS

Yosemite National Park provides habitat for many living things. Some have special status due to their dwindling numbers. "Special status" includes these categories:

ENDEMIC: An endemic species is unique to an area and lives nowhere else in the world. Yosemite has several examples of these, including the Mt. Lyell salamander, the Sierra Nevada yellow-legged frog, and the Yosemite toad.

YELLOW-LEGGED FROG

THREATENED: A threatened species is one that is likely to become endangered (see below) in the near future within all or much of its range. The Sierra Nevada red fox is one example of such a species in Yosemite.

NIGHTTIME VIEW OF A SIERRA NEVADA RED FOX, PHOTOGRAPHED WITH AN AUTOMATIC NIGHT MONITOR

GREAT GRAY OWL

ENDANGERED: Endangered species are at risk of becoming extinct throughout all or much of their range. Yosemite has several key species in this category, including the great gray owl and the Sierra Nevada bighorn.

EXTINCT: These species no longer exist in a particular region or, in some cases, anywhere in the world. The grizzly bear is extinct in California.

GRIZZLY BEARS STILL ROAM PARTS OF MONTANA, IDAHO, WASHINGTON, WYOMING, ALASKA, AND WESTERN CANADA

MANY MAMMALS

Yosemite has about ninety species of mammals: animals that have hair or fur and nurse their young. Here are some of the most exciting and interesting mammals you might get to see.

SQUIRRELS: This is probably the animal that park visitors most often see. There are five kinds of squirrels in Yosemite. The Douglas squirrel is a reddish color. The golden-mantled ground squirrel looks like a chipmunk because of the stripe on its back. The western gray squirrel has a long bushy tail. The Belding ground squirrel, also known as a "picket pin" for the way it stands up straight, can frequently be seen in the Tuolumne Meadows area. Yosemite's most common squirrel is the California ground squirrel, which is brown with white specks.

DEER: Mule deer get their name from their mule-like ears. These deer grow up to eighty inches long (more than six feet) from head to tail—the size of a very large dog—and can weigh up to 175 pounds. Mule deer are often seen in meadows, but they also dwell in forests. They forage on grasses and also nibble on twigs and leaves. Although they may seem gentle, never approach a deer! Deer attack people more often than bears do. Mule deer, if cornered or threatened, can charge and attack using their hooves and antlers.

CALIFORNIA GROUND SQUIRREL

MULE DEER

RACCOONS: Raccoons are up to two feet long, not counting their tails, which add another eight to twelve inches. They are gray to black in color, with a black mask around their eyes and black rings on their tails. Raccoons are common in Yosemite in the woods and near water. They are excellent climbers and often nest in trees. Raccoons are omnivores, eating anything from nuts, seeds, and fruit to eggs, insects, fish, and frogs. But they also are well known for getting into human food, which is one of many good reasons to store all food properly while you are in the park!

A FAMILY OF RACCOONS EATING IN THE WOODS

BIG BROWN BAT

BATS: There are seventeen species of bats that live in Yosemite. Bats avoid large temperature fluctuations, so they roost where temperatures remain some-what stable, such as in a rock crevice or a tree. Sequoia groves are prime roost-ing habitats for bats, as they find cavities within the trees to nestle in. And rock climbers who put their ears to cracks in the granite they are scaling sometimes hear spotted bats or mastiff bats squeaking in there somewhere! Another rea-son why bats colonize in these locations is that they are safe during the day from predators. Park visitors often see bats flitting about in the sky at twilight, when they become active, seeking out their prime food, insects—including mosquitos. The big brown bat is Yosemite's most common bat. The largest bat in the park is the western mastiff bat, which has a wingspan of over twenty-two inches. The smallest is the western pipistrelle, which weighs less than an ounce and has a wingspan of about eight inches.

SKUNKS: One common mammal in Yosemite that you might smell before you see is the striped skunk. This skunk is identified by the white-on-black stripes that run from its nose over its back to its tail. Skunks are about the size of house cats, weighing up to fourteen pounds. They are omnivores, eating berries and other plant foods as well as mice, eggs, insects, and carrion, or dead animals. They are most known for the foul odor they spray when they feel threatened.

STRIPED SKUNK

A COYOTE ENCOUNTERS A CAR

COYOTES: Coyotes are common in Yosemite. They are about the size of a collie, weighing from about twenty to forty-five pounds, and are typically gray to brownish. Visitors can sometimes identify their tracks and hear yipping or howling before they see coyotes. In the valley, coyotes are more likely to be seen in fall or winter, when it is less crowded.

MOUNTAIN LION

MOUNTAIN LIONS: Although rarely seen, mountain lions, also known as cougars, live within Yosemite. Ranging in habitat from the foothills up to 10,000 feet, mountain lions can weigh up to 150 pounds and grow to eight feet in length. Typically shy and isolated, when they are spotted they are usually on the prowl for raccoons, rodents, coyotes, or deer.

BOBCAT

BOBCATS: Bobcats are more likely to be seen in the park than mountain lions. These smaller mammals are most active before dawn and from sunset on into the evening for several hours. Bobcats are tan to grayish with black-tipped, pointed ears. They weigh up to thirty pounds and grow to forty inches long (between two and three feet). Bobcats eat rabbits, rodents, and even insects.

MARMOTS: An animal that visitors sometimes see sunbathing in the high country is the yellow-bellied marmot. Also known as a rock chuck, the marmot is part of the ground squirrel family and is actually a large rodent. Yosemite's marmots weigh between five and eleven pounds and live in colonies in rocky areas above 6,500 feet. Male marmots dig, or burrow, under rocks to stay safe from predators, providing a home for up to four females at a time. Each female may have a litter of four or five babies. When they sense danger, marmots whistle to warn other marmots nearby. Marmots are omnivores, eating grass, leaves, flowers, grasshoppers, and bird eggs. In Yosemite, high-country backpackers are most likely to see them, but other visitors often spot them at Olmsted Point, sunning on the rocks. The rocky area near Tioga Pass is also prime marmot habitat.

YELLOW-BELLIED MARMOT

PIKAS IN PERIL

The pika is a small relative of the rabbit. It lives in high, rocky areas near or above treeline. Pikas are shy creatures with short round ears, grayish to brown. They are often identified by the high-pitched whistling sound they make. Pikas are about six to eight inches tall and weigh only four to six ounces—less than half a pound. Pikas eat mostly grasses, herbs, and flowers. Because they live in the high mountains, food is very difficult to find in winter. They survive by cutting and sun-drying food in hay piles in the summer and storing it for the winter.

Pikas in Yosemite are facing new challenges. They live in cool, moist areas near mountaintops, in areas where climate change is causing temperatures to be higher than they used to be. Pikas have thick fur and are highly active during the warmest months of the year, eating and gathering food. They do not burrow and instead use natural rock piles to hide in. This means that they cannot hide from temperatures too warm for them. They have a hard time trying to migrate to cooler areas farther north because they would have to leave the mountains and go through warmer, lower elevations to get there. As a result, pikas are stuck on "sky islands" with few options for getting away from a warming climate. Several pika populations have disappeared from their habitats.

A PIKA GATHERS HAY

SIERRA NEVADA BIGHORN SHEEP

AN INTERVIEW WITH YOSEMITE WILDLIFE BIOLOGIST
STEVE THOMPSON

Q: WHEN WERE THE BIGHORN EXTINCT IN YOSEMITE?

A: These impressive animals were extinct in the park until the mid-1980s. That's when twenty-six bighorn were reintroduced just outside the park, in the hope that they'll eventually reoccupy their historical habitat back within Yosemite's boundaries.

Q: WHERE DO YOSEMITE'S BIGHORNS LIVE NOW?

A: There are two herds of bighorns, one living in the vicinity of Mt. Gibbs and the other spreading northward along Tioga Pass and Warren Crest and across Lundy Canyon. The approximately forty total sheep in these areas are descendants of the ones that were released near the park in 1986 and 1988.

YOSEMITE PARK RANGER STEVE THOMPSON

Q: WHY WERE THEY GONE IN THE FIRST PLACE?

A: Sierra Nevada bighorns were missing from the Yosemite area for two main reasons. One was that they were frequently hunted for food during the mining era. But the main reason was that the bighorns were being exposed to diseases brought into the region by domestic sheep, and that essentially wiped them out. Recently the state and federal governments have listed Sierra Nevada bighorns as an endangered species. This has helped establish a recovery plan and a series of actions to increase the number of bighorns. Mountain lions are another threat. The lions not only prey on the sheep but force them to winter at high altitude, where food is scarce, which can cause a high winter mortality rate (death rate).

Q: WHAT ARE THE CHANCES THAT AN AVERAGE VISITOR WILL SPOT ONE?

A: It is very rare that Yosemite visitors spot these noble-looking animals, as they are often far from roads, grazing at high elevations near the eastern side of the park.

THE FAMOUS BLACK BEAR

Despite the abundant wildlife, Yosemite's most famous animal by far is the black bear. There are about three hundred to five hundred black bears living in the park. Although they are called black bears, they can be black, brown, or cinnamon-colored, with males weighing up to 350 pounds. They have an acute sense of smell, perhaps stronger than any other mammal's. They can actually detect food, such as a deer carcass, from several miles away! They gorge on berries in the summer and devour acorns in the fall. Bears also tear apart insect-infested logs and swallow hordes of ants and termites. Though it is well known that bears will eat food that humans bring into the park, it is always best that bears eat natural, wild food. Yosemite's bears live at all of the park's elevations. This includes forests, meadows, and high-elevation rocky areas. Bears are active at night but are often seen moving about in daytime as well. Park visitors should report all bear sightings.

A BLACK BEAR IN EARLY SPRING

A BEAR CUB CLINGS TO A TREE

HSC Employee / Other

ranger)

LOCATION: _____

REPORTING PARTY: Visitor / Resident / Ranger / HSC Employee / Oth

Name: _____

Address (optional): _____   Work Unit (if ranger)

e of a bear with both Roto
and Allflex tags

Example of a bear with bo
and Allflex tags

WERE BEARS SEEN? Yes / No

HOW MANY BEARS?
Adults _____
Cubs _____
Yearlings _____

Allflex
Tag

Roto
Tag

RADIO COLLAR: Yes / No / Unknown

EAR TAGS: Yes / No / Unknown

ircle if any)

NUMBER ON TAG (if known): _____

wn

Roto / Allflex   (circle if any)

nknown

EAR TAG LOCATION: Left Ear / Right Ear / Both Ears / Unknown

n / Blonde

EAR TAG COLOR: Green / Blue / Yellow / White / Orange / Unknown

COLOR OF BEAR: Black / Dark Brown / Med. Brown / Light Brown / Blonde

DESCRIBE THE BEAR(S) AND THEIR BEHAVIOR: _____

_____

_____

_____

this report

Please

The Smartest Bears in the World

Black bears in Yosemite are so skilled at breaking into cars that they have been called "the smartest bears in the world." Bears have excellent vision and can detect color in ice chests, groceries, and food containers. If food has been left in a vehicle, bears will break windows, bend door frames, and pry open camper shells. They even can get inside a car and pry open the trunk through the backseat! Bears caused over $80,000 in property damage in 2009, in more than 450 incidents. You can imagine what a bear-damaged car looks like.

All parking lots and trailheads in the park have bear-proof lockers where food and anything else with a scent, such as cosmetics, can be stored without the worry of a bear break-in. At night, no food can be stored in vehicles. During the day, food can be left in the car as long as it is out of sight and the windows are closed. Visitors should also be careful with food at picnic tables. Bears have been known to come right up to a table, searching for an easy meal. Storing food properly is required by law. Failure to comply can cost a bear's life and it can also cost up to $5,000 in fines.

A BEAR BREAKS INTO A CAR

Night Bear Patrol

Bear activity peaks in August, the time of year when there are the most visitors to the park. But park rangers are taking action to reduce the number of problems. In 2009 bear-management rangers in Yosemite completed over two hundred night patrols, inspected thousands of cars and campsites, and gave thousands of warnings, levied fines, and enforced campsite cleanup orders for improper food storage. They also trapped twenty-one bears and radio-collared twelve others. The battle to protect people and bears is ongoing.

Bear Canisters

It used to be that backcountry hikers in Yosemite were told to hang their food from a tree using a counterbalance method. But determined bears with a powerful sense of smell (a hundred times stronger than a dog's) have found ways to climb the trees and get into the food anyway. Now all backcountry campers in Yosemite must use bear canisters. These highly durable, bear-resistant containers are for all food items and anything else with a scent. Bears soon learn that the cylinder-shaped canisters are not worth dealing with. The canisters are the only effective method of preventing bears from getting human food in the wilderness. Canisters can be rented at all Yosemite backcountry permit offices.

DID YOU KNOW?

Late in the summer, bears can eat up to 20,000 calories each day. That's a lot of food when you consider that you and I usually consume only 2,000 to 3,000 calories a day. The largest bear ever captured and weighed at Yosemite tipped the scales at 690 pounds!

BEAR MANAGEMENT

AN INTERVIEW WITH YOSEMITE WILDLIFE BIOLOGIST
TORI SEHER

Q: HOW DO BEARS BECOME PROBLEM BEARS?

A: We don't like to call bears "problems," because the problem really is with people and food storage. But there are two ways bears can become issues. One is that they become habituated. That means they are used to people and often look for food without being bothered by people nearby. So the bears get too close to developed areas. The other is that they become food-conditioned. That is when bears learn that people mean food, and they'll seek out food in trash cans and in camping areas. Some bears can become both food-conditioned and habituated.

Q: HOW ARE BEARS MANAGED TO KEEP THEM AWAY FROM HUMAN AREAS?

YOSEMITE PARK RANGER TORI SEHER

A: The best way to do this is proper food storage. Even if we chase them away, they will come back. There are rangers that patrol campgrounds and other areas at night with rubber slugs and clear paintballs, and also yell at them. We teach the bears to stay at least fifty yards from a developed area. Some of the bears now know us and our truck and get past that fifty-yard mark as soon as they see us, or better yet, stay at that perimeter boundary once they have learned what to expect. Bears learn quickly! But a bear's drive for food is incredibly strong, so we must remain vigilant in keeping bears away from human food. Bears are constantly testing these boundaries! We also trap bears by placing meat or fish or even fruit in a trap to lure them in. Then we immobilize them and tag their ears so we can monitor the bear, sometimes with a radio collar. Colored tags are put on their ears, but the colors are random, they don't mean anything.

Q: WHAT ARE SOME OF THE MOST PROBLEMATIC AREAS OF THE PARK?

A: This often varies year to year. But the most incidents typically occur in the valley. White Wolf and Tuolumne Meadows are also often high bear incident areas.

Q: WHAT SHOULD A VISITOR DO WHEN SPOTTING A BEAR?

A. Certainly keep your distance and never turn your back on your food. Once you are done eating and cleaning up, store all scented items properly! Don't walk away from the food, even temporarily. It should always be within an arm's reach. Also, bears often can be scared away aggressively. Make noise and shout to chase them off. And report all bear sightings to a ranger. We like to know where they are.

Q: DO YOU KNOW OF ANY UNUSUAL RECENT BEAR INCIDENTS?

A: Yes, actually, these things are always going on. But last year a bear got into a car that was parked on a slant. When it got in, the door slammed shut due to the angle the car was parked on, and the bear couldn't get out. The next day the owner of the car, a woman, came to it in the morning to take off driving, but there was a 350-pound bear sleeping in the backseat!

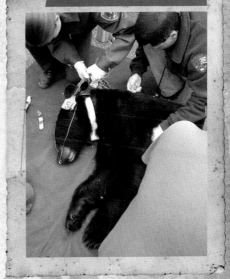

A BEAR BEING TAGGED

Quick Tips
FOR KEEPING BEARS SAFE

Yosemite's black bears are a treasure and the park is their home. But human behaviors are hurting some of the bears. Here are a few ways we can help protect them:

- Store all food properly. When bears get human food, problems often follow.

- If you see a bear at close range, scare it away by yelling and making noise. Children should stay close to adults.

- People should drive only as fast as the speed limit. Speeding kills bears and other animals.

- Report all bear sightings to a ranger. Bear incident report forms are available at visitor centers.

- Also report to a ranger any unusual activity between visitors and bears.

MAKE NOISE IF A BEAR APPROACHES YOU

Here, Have Some Garbage!

Starting in the 1940s, Yosemite food waste was dumped into large, open garbage dumpsters or areas called "bear pits." People then would gather around to watch the bears eat. The bear pits not only provided entertainment but were also a way to lure bears away from campgrounds and lodging areas. Later the Park Service realized that this practice was bad for people and for the bears. Bears learned that food meant people, and they started aggressively going after food from park visitors. Some people got injured and cars were damaged by bears breaking into them. Some bears had to be killed. The practice of using open garbage bins ended in 1971. Since then, *all* food—and that includes garbage—must be stored overnight in bear-proof lockers, which are located throughout the park.

DID YOU KNOW?

Yosemite's bears hibernate for the winter. They hide out in hollowed trees or logs or in rock caves. While in hibernation, a bear has a low body temperature and slow heart rate. This conserves energy. Hibernating bears don't go to the bathroom during their extended rest. They do wander out once in a while, though, so it isn't impossible to see a black bear in Yosemite in winter.

ALL FOOD—AND THAT INCLUDES GARBAGE—MUST BE STORED OVERNIGHT IN BEAR-PROOF LOCKERS, WHICH ARE LOCATED THROUGHOUT THE PARK.

We checked in at the camp early in the afternoon. When I was setting up my family's tent a ranger came by and warned, "There was a bear in your site last night. He's been coming around every night, ever since someone left out a cooler. I just wanted to let you know." The ranger drove off and my wife and I looked at each other, wondering what the night had in store. We spent the day in the park and came back to camp for dinner. As it got dark, we cleaned up, put *everything* away in the bear locker, and got into the tent.

Around 10 p.m., just as I was about to doze off, I heard several people scream "Bear!" My family and I immediately sat up. The commotion outside grew. We heard more shouts of "Bear, get out of here!" and "Go! Shoo!" There were also flashlights shining about. We all hurried out of our pajamas, got into our clothes, and stepped outside. The large gathering of people were pointing their flashlights near our tent and yelling. The loud, aggressive group reminded me of villagers with torches chasing Frankenstein in the movies.

AUTHOR MIKE GRAF AND HIS WIFE, KIMBERLY ALEXANDER

"Where is it?" I called down to the crowd that was blinding us with their lights. "Right behind you!" was the reply. We turned, and sure enough, ten feet up on a stump was the culprit, looking down at the gathering and wondering what its next move would be. My wife and I grabbed our two-year-old daughter and shuffled barefoot into the safety of the mass of people while everyone continued to shout at the bear. I should mention that it's Yosemite policy to scare away bears. I had learned that from the ranger earlier in the day. But this time the bear wasn't budging. Food-conditioned bears, I understand, are hard to deal with. A ranger truck drove up. Two rangers jumped out with paintball guns pointed. They dashed up the hill, shouting at the bear and shooting the gun once they were within range. This time the bear tore off up the hill. Soon they were out of sight, and then a moment later, "BOOM!" a gun went off. I instantly felt sick to my stomach as the explosion echoed throughout camp. *They killed the bear due to a camper's carelessness,* I thought. The two rangers walked back down. "Sorry for the noise," one said to the group. Then she added, "Paintballs and yelling are just not working for this bear. Neither are relocations. It keeps coming back. So we set off a firecracker. It's gone now." I let out my breath. The bear was okay.

After the incident we all filed back to our campsites—my family and I didn't have to go more than just a few feet. Our daughter slept between my wife and me in the tent that night. That is, if you could call it sleep. We heard shouts of "bear" around different parts of the campground all night long. That is one persistent bear! We had two nights reserved at Crane Flat. The next night, after dinner, we gathered into the tent, expecting the same thing. But this time all was quiet until around 5 a.m. Then we were awakened by coyotes yapping!

"...IT'S YOSEMITE POLICY TO SCARE AWAY BEARS. I HAD LEARNED THAT FROM THE RANGER..."

— MIKE GRAF

SPEED KILLS

A Red Bear sign program recently began with the goal of stopping collisions between bears and cars, which are all too frequent in Yosemite. Now there are warning signs posted throughout the park with pictures of red bears on them, marking locations where cars have struck bears. Despite the signs, in 2009 twenty-five bears were hit by cars in Yosemite. Seventeen were hit in 2008. An unknown number of deer, squirrels, and other park animals were also struck. Yosemite park rangers are hoping that drivers will obey speed limits while in the park, and fewer bears will be hit.

SPEEDING KILLS BEARS

THESE SIGNS MARK WHERE BEARS HAVE BEEN HIT IN YOSEMITE

AMPHIBIANS AND REPTILES

Amphibians are capable of living on land and in water while breathing through their skin. There are twelve species of amphibians in Yosemite, including frogs, toads, newts, and salamanders. Amphibians are cold-blooded: they need to be in the sun to warm themselves. That's why frogs are sometimes spotted basking on rocks near water.

There are twenty-two reptile species in Yosemite. Like amphibians, reptiles, which include turtles, lizards, and snakes, are cold-blooded. The western pond turtle is the only turtle species in the park. There are eight species of lizards, with the western fence lizard being the most commonly seen. For snakes it's the garter snake.

WESTERN FENCE LIZARD: If you see a lizard doing push-ups, it's a fence lizard. The male lizard does push-ups or bobs his head to attract a mate. If two males are doing push-ups near each other, it is a threat. They are having a dispute over their territory that may lead to a fight, with one leaving the area.

WESTERN FENCE LIZARD IN PUSH-UP POSITION

RATTLESNAKE: The western rattlesnake is Yosemite's only poisonous vertebrate animal. Although they are venomous and can cause severe injuries and (rarely) death, they are also shy and withdrawn. Rattlers live in the region from the San Joaquin Valley plains to the foothills, and all the way up to about 8,000 feet elevation. They can get up to three to four feet in length but are often much smaller. They spend a great deal of their time in a slow, lethargic mode, often in the sun on a rock outcrop. This includes cleared trails and it isn't that unusual for a hiker to turn a corner and see one right on the path. So watch your step and take

WESTERN RATTLESNAKE

care not to walk where you can't see the ground. Always step on rocks or logs and never over them, in case a snake is on the other side. Be careful not to put your hands or feet anywhere you can't see. Typically, in an encounter with a human, a rattler will glide into nearby bushes within a few moments if it is left alone. Only when cornered are they likely to strike. It is recommended that you back off from the snake and let it retreat.

GO SEE IT! The Nature Center at Happy Isles is along the way to the Mist Trail to Vernal Fall, at the end of the valley. The nature center has dioramas of day and night animals of the forest and their sounds. Animals featured include bears, owls, skunks, weasels, bats, porcupines, and mountain lions, among others. The scat and print exhibit teaches you how to identify footprints and droppings of deer, owls, bears, bobcats, and coyotes. You can also monitor earthquake activity and check the weather at the gauging station nearby.

AN ABUNDANCE OF BIRDS

Tweet! Tweet! Here are some of the two hundred species of birds you may end up seeing as you enjoy the park. Mornings are the best time to see birds at Yosemite, away from crowds.

BIRD IDENTIFICATION GUIDE
BIRDS OFTEN SEEN

American robin

Acorn woodpecker

Black-headed grosbeak

Clark's nutcracker

Common raven

Mountain chickadee

Red-tailed hawk

Steller's jay

American dipper
(water ouzel)

LESS COMMONLY SEEN BIRDS

Spotted owl

Peregrine falcon

Pileated woodpecker

Northern goshawk

BROWN-HEADED COWBIRD

A CRUEL TRICK

A non-native bird, the brown-headed cowbird, has caused a decline in a number of bird species in the park. Cowbirds lay their eggs in other birds' nests, alongside the eggs that belong there. The cowbirds often hatch first, getting a head start on feeding. Sometimes they even shove the other eggs out of the nest. The willow flycatcher and some other species of songbirds are examples of birds whose numbers have been affected by cowbirds.

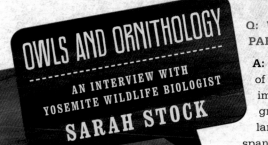

OWLS AND ORNITHOLOGY

AN INTERVIEW WITH YOSEMITE WILDLIFE BIOLOGIST
SARAH STOCK

Q: WHAT IS YOUR CHIEF ROLE AT THE PARK?

A: My specialty is ornithology, or the study of birds. One of the most fascinating and important birds we are studying is the great gray owl. This unique bird is the largest owl in North America, with a wingspan of around five feet. This is approaching the arm span of adult humans when holding their arms fully extended to the side.

Q: HOW MANY GREAT GRAY OWLS ARE THERE IN YOSEMITE?

A: The great gray owl is a state-listed endangered bird, and only one of three endangered bird species within the park. We just completed a three-year study to learn more about these amazing birds. This study is helping us to get a further idea for how many great gray owls live in the Yosemite region. Our results so far show that there is about a 66 percent, or two-thirds, chance that a mid-elevation park meadow will be occupied by a great gray owl. But it is rare that these owls are seen in Yosemite Valley, due to all the crowds.

YOSEMITE PARK RANGER SARAH STOCK

Q: HOW CAN A VISITOR POSSIBLY SEE ONE?

A: The best way to try and spot one is to find a quiet location at the edge of a meadow at dawn or dusk and wait patiently, while sitting still for an hour or more. What is more likely is that a visitor may see a sign of an owl within a suitable habitat. They drop pellet balls of fur and bones, called owl pellets, where they eat. Their primary prey are voles and pocket gophers. Another unique thing about Yosemite's great gray owl is that they are isolated in Yosemite. 75 percent of the great gray owl population in California is only here in this park!

Q: WHAT OTHER SPECIAL BIRDS ARE THERE?

A: Another special bird in Yosemite is the peregrine falcon. Their primary habitat is the cliffs the park is famous for. These birds were nearly wiped out in the 1970s due to the chemical DDT getting into their systems, causing their eggs to not be hard enough to be able to develop a baby chick. But they made a tremendous comeback in Yosemite once they were reintroduced into the park during a recovery period. One way scientists helped the peregrine was to raise viable, or able-to-hatch, eggs in labs and replace the too-soft eggs in a peregrine's nest with them. The adults then raised and incubated the replacement egg as if it was one of their own.

Peregrines live on some of the cliffs that our rock climbers scale. Due to this there are sometimes closures of certain rock faces because of nesting activity, and this is being constantly monitored and updated.

Q: ARE THERE ANY OTHER UNIQUE ANIMAL SPECIES YOU ARE MONITORING CLOSELY?

A: The park is the habitat for the yellow-legged frog. Only 5 percent of these amphibians remain, although, according to John Muir, they were once one of the most abundant alpine species within the park. They live in higher-elevation waters, such as areas around Tuolumne Meadows, but non-native fish have decimated the frogs, as these fish eat the tadpoles.

Despite all of Yosemite's wildlife challenges, I feel very fortunate to live and work in a place like this.

OBSERVING WILDLIFE: A SPECIAL GUIDE

Special Signs

Sometimes we don't see wildlife but there are clues that they have been in the area. Here are some of the most unique or interesting wildlife clues:

Voles, Ground Squirrels, and Gophers: In meadows look for burrows or mounds. Voles and ground squirrels make burrows in grassy areas, and pocket gophers create mounds. These small animals are an important food source for nearly all the predators in the park, including the great gray owl.

Douglas Squirrels: Douglas squirrels climb trees to get to cones. Once they have one, they tear it apart and drop the shredded cone remnants or shavings to the forest floor.

Bears: Bears often scratch their claws against trees in the park. These claw marks are a good sign that a bear has crossed this path!

Bats: Rock climbers often scale the same rocks that bats roost in. Sometimes these bats leave behind small piles of their droppings, called guano.

Owls: Yosemite's owls often nest and hunt in and around the park's meadows and forests. Look for owl pellets: small balls of fur mixed with bones. This is what owls spit up after digesting their food.

Pikas: Pikas can sometimes be spotted on talus slopes in the park's high country. But you are more likely to see a hay pile that a pika has left for itself to eat during the long, snowy winter!

Woodpeckers: Woodpeckers drill holes in tree trunks while searching for insects. These small holes become homes for other animals once the woodpecker has left. Be on the lookout for trees with lots of holes in them.

Deer: Deer and bears often lie in the grass. Look for flattened areas in grassy meadows where these large animals have been resting.

Bighorn Sheep: Bighorn sheep are seldom spotted. But a backcountry explorer might notice where sheep have pawed a rough gravel area and made a soft dirt bed to lie down in.

Snakes: Snakes shed their skins and sometimes visitors encounter these leftover skins. The snake skins you are most likely to see are from the park's most common snakes—garter, king, and western rattler.

Tracks

Many animals leave tracks in dirt, or in sand near riverbanks. Here are some of the most common tracks seen:

Deer

Bear

Raccoon

Coyote

Bobcat

Raven

Feathers

Birds often leave behind feathers. It is not unusual to see raven or Steller's jay feathers in Yosemite Valley.

Raven   Steller's jay

Scat

An animal's scat (or poo!) is a common sign that animals have crossed a path. Here are different kinds of animal scat:

Bear   Deer   Raccoon

Bobcat   Marmot

Please, Please, Please Don't Feed the Animals!

In Yosemite it is illegal to harm wildlife in any way. This includes approaching to cause harm, as well as hunting, collecting, or feeding. If you see people feeding animals in the park, please report it to the rangers. Yosemite park rangers ask all visitors not to approach wildlife and to keep their distance even if the wildlife approaches them. Dispose of all trash properly in animal-proof trash cans or dumpsters. And store all food properly, day and night.

There are several reasons why it is not okay to feed wildlife. In addition to being illegal and subject to a fine of up to $5,000, feeding wild animals:

- Increases their food supply artificially. This sometimes causes animals to have larger litters of babies, but the available amount of wild food can't sustain their larger families.

- Is unhealthy for them. Wild animals have specialized, natural diets. Human food can harm the health and growth of any wild animal.

- Causes them to lose their natural fear of humans. Animals may get hurt if they get too close to people.

- Could cause them to hurt someone. Wild animals have sharp teeth, claws, talons, and spines, as well as venom and other toxins that are part of their natural line of defense. These could be harmful or even fatal if used against a human. And some animals that seem harmless, like chipmunks, don't necessarily know where someone's fingers end and the food begins.

- Lures animals into areas populated by humans. This leads to more problems between people and wildlife. It also changes their natural, patterned behavior for finding food.

- Could injure or kill them. It's not just the food that is unhealthy: animals that eat human food also end up eating plastic wrappers and other food containers that could kill them.

YES, EVEN ME!

Sometimes humans who don't understand that the squirrels in the park are wild animals feed them. This causes problems for both squirrels and people; squirrels can become sick from human food, and visitors can be bitten and scratched by squirrels who have lost their fear of humans. Please do not feed them!

Wildlife Encounters: What Do We Do Now?

What visitors should do when they encounter an animal depends on the situation. Here are a few possibilities:

You are hiking out of the Wawona area and your family spots a mountain lion about a hundred yards away. It appears to be looking right at you.

The group should gather together to look as large as possible. Small children should sit on the shoulders of adults. Watch the mountain lion closely, keeping eye contact. If it follows or looks aggressive, leave the area slowly without running. You should also wave your arms, throw small objects at it, and shout in a low-pitched voice. A high-pitched squeal resembles that of a deer being attacked by a mountain lion, and that reminds them of prey, possibly making them more aggressive. If the lion attacks, fight back in any way you can, including throwing sticks or rocks. The goal is to show the lion that *you* are dangerous to *it*. Report all sightings immediately to a ranger.

You are picnicking in the valley and a large bear lumbers into the vicinity. The bear wanders closer and jumps up on a picnic table nearby, then licks the table.

Gather up all your food and slowly leave the area. If the bear continues to get closer, shout and bang pots to chase it off. Children should stay close to adults. Don't run. Report the sighting.

You pull over at Olmsted Point and a large marmot rambles over to you. The animal continues to get closer and closer, obviously seeking a handout of the snacks you and your family are eating.

Shoo off the marmot and don't let it get too close—it might bite! Never feed it!

THE GOAL IS TO SHOW THE LION THAT YOU ARE DANGEROUS TO IT.

A MOUNTAIN LION BARES ITS FANGS

THE WORLD'S SMARTEST BEARS AND OTHER FASCINATING WILDLIFE

RAFTING ON THE MERCED RIVER

7

WATER, WATER EVERYWHERE

Yosemite is in the heart of the Sierra Nevada, a four-hundred-mile-long mountain range. In fact, "Sierra Nevada" is actually Spanish for "snowy mountain range." Over five hundred inches of snow fall in some parts of the Sierra annually. In the spring this massive snowpack melts, feeding many streams, lakes, and rivers, including those of Yosemite.

RIVERS AND LAKES

Of the hundreds of creeks, streams, and rivers in Yosemite, two of the most seen are the Tuolumne River, which feeds into Hetch Hetchy Reservoir, and the Merced River, which runs right through Yosemite Valley. Yosemite has many backcountry lakes of all sizes, but the best-known is Tenaya Lake, right next to Tioga Road. Another popular lake is Mirror Lake, which got its name from the reflections it once displayed, particularly of Half Dome. Now the lake is being filled in with sediment, so the famous reflections are mostly gone. But there are still places to swim, explore, hike, and hang out, with tremendous views of Half Dome far above. The valley bus system drops visitors off just down the hill from Mirror Lake. From there it is about a one-mile walk on a paved road up to the lake.

GO SEE IT!

Rafting the Merced River might be one of the best ways to see the valley, with each bend in the river leading to a new and wonderful view. Sandbars and beaches are appealing places to swim, rest, and picnic. Yosemite's raft season depends on snowmelt, water temperature, and the river's depth. The conditions are usually best from late May until late July, and rafts can be rented at Curry Village. The fees for each raft include a three-mile trip down the river and the shuttle back.

GO SEE IT! If your family is driving along Tioga Road, try to take time to picnic along Tenaya Lake's shoreline. The clear sparkling waters and massive granite formations surrounding the lake make for perfect scenery while you have your lunch.

WATERFALLS

The word "waterfall" means "plunging water that drops in one or more places." A perfect example of multiple drops is Yosemite Falls, with its three very distinct sections. The top part of the falls drops 1,430 feet, or about the height of Chicago's Sears Tower. The second plunge, which is called the Middle Cascade, drops 675 feet. Lower Yosemite Falls drops an additional 320 feet, or about the length of a soccer field. In total, the falls plunge 2,425 feet, about the height of the Eiffel Tower plus the Sears Tower. Bridalveil Fall, on the other hand, is one continuous fall of 620 feet.

Much of what flows into Yosemite Falls is from the winter snowpack, which falls onto bare granite and begins to melt in the spring. There are few water storage areas—lakes, ponds, or streams—and little soil for water to sink into along this drainage, so Yosemite Falls often dries up late in summer. A much smaller watershed feeds Bridalveil Fall, but it is a year-round waterfall—it never goes completely dry. This is because its watershed is over forest and meadows on north-facing slopes.

Yosemite's waterfalls are best seen during late spring, when melting snow creates peak flow. This usually is in mid-May or early June. By late summer or fall, there is little or no snowpack and little rain in the high country, so many of the park's waterfalls dry up.

When visiting waterfalls, remember that nearby rocks are wet and very slippery. Never swim at the top of a waterfall.

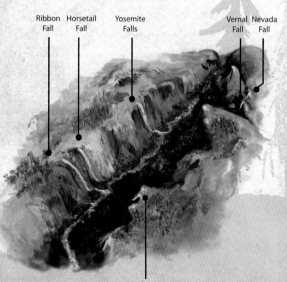

Ribbon Fall   Horsetail Fall   Yosemite Falls   Vernal Fall   Nevada Fall

Bridalveil Fall

Famous Falls

YOSEMITE FALLS: This is the tallest waterfall in North America and the fifth tallest in the world. This iconic 2,425-foot plunge of water, the park's most famous, is easily seen from Yosemite Valley roads, the Yosemite Lodge, or the short, flat trail to the base of the falls. If you are fit and adventurous you can climb the steep Yosemite Falls Trail all the way to the top, with close-up views along the way of the three sections of plunging water. Once you are at the top, head over to the railing that overlooks the whole waterfall.

BRIDALVEIL FALL: This 620-foot, free-flowing drop typically runs all year and can be easily seen from the Wawona Tunnel over-look. But for a close-up view, take the short walk at the waterfall's trailhead—just be prepared to get wet!

VERNAL FALL: Another year-round producer, Vernal Fall drops 317 feet, right next to the very popular Mist Trail—and it is called "Mist Trail" for a reason. You should be prepared for a shower, especially early in the summer!

NEVADA FALL: Farther up the Mist Trail, Nevada Fall plunges 594 feet. It is a steep hike to the top, but well worth it.

HORSETAIL FALL: This 1,000-foot fall runs through spring, plunging off the east face of El Capitan.

RIBBON FALL: This 1,612-foot drop of water (pictured here) is best seen from March until June. It is visible while driving into the valley just beyond the Bridalveil Fall turnoff.

CHILNUALNA FALLS: The sight of a 240-foot drop awaits those who hike the Chilnualna Falls trail out of the Wawona area. But it is hard to see the whole waterfall behind the rocks. Still, there are some great cascades, sometimes called Lower Chilnualna Falls, near the beginning of the trail.

In addition to all the falls mentioned above, there are even more to see: Waterwheel Falls, in the high country out of Tuolumne Meadows; Rancheria Falls, well past Wapama Falls out of Hetch Hetchy; Tueeulala Falls, a fantastic plunge along the trail to Wapama Falls; and Snow Creek Falls, past Mirror Lake and near a steep trail into the high country. Less often visited, Illilouette Fall flows all year. A small section of the waterfall can be viewed along the way to Vernal Fall before the mist section. For a better view, take the Panorama Trail down from Glacier Point right to the top of the falls. Wapama Falls is another less-often-seen waterfall, but if you take the time to see it, you are in for a treat! Wapama Falls drops 1,400 feet into Hetch Hetchy Reservoir, and the trail goes right to a footbridge looking up at it. Be prepared to get soaked in early season!

THE TOP OF CHILNUALNA FALLS

GO SEE IT! If you get up to Glacier Point and take in the famous view, among the sights that greet you will be the sheer drops of Nevada Fall and Vernal Fall far below. Some people have referred to these two impressive drops as a "grand stairway" leading from the high country down to the valley.

MOONBOWS AT YOSEMITE FALLS

In his 1912 book, *The Yosemite*, John Muir wrote of "moonbows," which can be observed on spring nights when there is plenty of moonlight and a lot of run-off from the spring snowmelt. A lunar rainbow at Yosemite Falls, Muir wrote, is a "grand arc of color...amid the rush and roar and tumultuous dashing of this thunder-voiced fall" and "one of the most impressive and most cheering of all the blessed mountain evangels."

A MOONBOW AT YOSEMITE FALLS

A WATERFALL ON FIRE?

Horsetail Fall has a golden, fiery glow when it is lit by the setting sun during the last two weeks of February. Where do you see it? From a small meadow between Yosemite Lodge and El Capitan—you'll know the spot when you see all the other people there to witness this spectacular phenomenon.

HORSETAIL FALL ON "FIRE"

DID YOU KNOW?

The highest waterfall in the world is Angel Falls, in Venezuela, at 3,230 feet. Yosemite Falls, at 2,425 feet, is the highest in North America.

EXTREME H$_2$O

The Beauty That Can Kill

Although Yosemite's rivers, lakes, and waterfalls are beautiful, they are also unbelievably dangerous. Yosemite park rangers ask all visitors to do the following when swimming, rafting, or wading in rivers or lakes:

- Make sure everyone in the group sticks together and keeps an eye out for one another.
- Choose swim areas carefully and swim only in low water conditions.
- Avoid whitewater or areas where the water flows in and around rocks.
- Never swim or wade upstream from a waterfall. This includes Emerald Pools above Vernal Fall!
- Be wary of strong currents and icy water.
- Use bridges whenever possible to cross streams, creeks, and rivers. Stream-polished rocks are slippery, whether they are wet or dry.
- Wear flotation devices when rafting.
- Avoid fallen trees or debris in the water. They are hazardous to swimmers and rafters.
- Finally, for rafters: make sure the Merced River is open to rafting before you partake—check conditions first! Also, enter and exit the river only at designated launch and removal locations.

RUSHING WATER AT THE TOP OF YOSEMITE FALLS

A FLOODED YOSEMITE CAMPGROUND, 1997

The Worst Flood Ever

From January 1 to January 3, 1997, Yosemite Valley experienced the worst flood in the park's recent history. Flooding is a common, natural experience for Yosemite but the 1997 flood devastated the man-made areas of the park. The cause of the massive flood was heavy snowpack in the high country followed by warm temperatures and torrential rains from a tropical storm that pushed the snow level to above 8,000 feet. It rained all the way up at Tuolumne Meadows, at 8,600 feet, in the middle of winter, which is very unusual. The valley was closed to visitors from January 1 until March 14. Seven and a half miles of El Portal Road were washed out. The road was so damaged that it stayed closed until Memorial Day. The valley lost about half of its nine hundred campsites and many housing units. Over half of the valley's accommodations were left with severe flood damage. Thirty-three backcountry bridges were damaged as well. Luckily, nobody was killed. In the end, the Park Service relocated many of its buildings and campgrounds out of the river's floodplain or removed them altogether, knowing that this natural occurrence would happen again.

AFTER THE FLOOD

AN ACCOUNT FROM YOSEMITE PARK RANGER AND ASSISTANT SUPERINTENDENT FOR PUBLIC AND LEGISLATIVE AFFAIRS

SCOTT GEDIMAN

The image I remember most is that there was water everywhere you turned, with waterfalls all over the place. And the width and strength of the waterfalls were unreal. Yosemite Falls was shooting straight out from the top. Once the floodwaters receded, which really began after a few days, I remember how quiet the park was. It was closed, so the only ones here were us rangers, emergency crews, and the press. I even recall how much more wildlife was around. I saw bobcats, deer, and coyote more frequently. But destruction was everywhere. Roads looked like what I describe as "smashed graham crackers." There were also canvas tents on top of cars, cars on their sides, picnic tables turned over and in the river. There were flood lines marked on buildings, too, when the water level went down. We have now marked high-water areas throughout the valley. But all the natural features of the park were fine. Yosemite has been going through events like this for eons. Those of us who remained at the park dealt with the damaged buildings, sewer system, electricity, water lines, and such. There was a great deal of camaraderie developed among the crew involved. And there was lots to deal with—about $400 million in property damage. We were finally able to reopen the valley on March 14.

WATER, WATER EVERYWHERE

137

HIGHWAY 140 AFTER 1997 FLOOD DAMAGE

GO SEE IT! There are high-water signs all around the valley showing how high the water got during the 1997 flood. Look for these as you travel around and try to imagine how high the water was for the first three days of January 1997.

8 ENDLESS THINGS TO SEE AND DO

Yosemite has something to offer everyone. Whether it be swimming, hiking, backpacking, art classes, cooking by a campfire, cultural events, biking, or sitting among some towering sequoias and reading, there is something to do at the park no matter what your interests are.

TAKE A HIKE!

With about eight hundred miles of trails within the park—about the length of the state of California—there are a multitude of hikes to choose from. The easy trails listed here are mostly flat. Hikes that are listed as moderate have some hills and high altitude. The difficult trails involve major climbs on uneven terrain, often at high elevations.

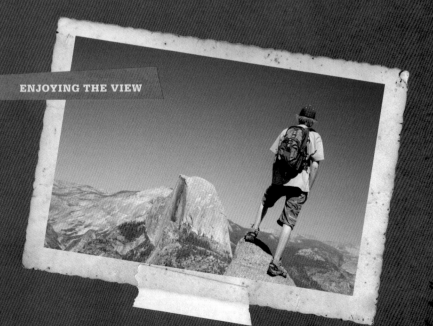

ENJOYING THE VIEW

Easy Trails

MIRROR LAKE AND TENAYA CANYON: A mostly flat trail at the east end of the valley, one mile to Mirror Lake and then farther into Tenaya Canyon. Streamside and forested, this is a very scenic walk and great for picnicking.

TUOLUMNE MEADOWS: Short hikes of varying distances lead into the meadows. It's about 0.75 miles from the trailhead to Soda Springs, where cold, carbonated water bubbles out of the ground (but is not safe to drink!). Please stay on trails in the meadows.

Moderate Trails

MARIPOSA GROVE OF SEQUOIAS AND MUSEUM: Many trail options exist in the grove, winding their way through the sequoias at the southwest part of the park. The Grizzly Giant is a popular option and is 1.6 miles, round trip. The museum is about 2 miles from the trailhead, depending on which way you go.

SENTINEL DOME: This spectacular high-country hike near Glacier Point leads to views overlooking the valley. From the trailhead to the commanding Sentinel Dome, it's 2.2 miles with longer loop options, including Taft Point.

Difficult Trails

MIST TRAIL TO VERNAL FALL AND NEVADA FALL: One of the park's most popular trails begins at Happy Isles, in Yosemite Valley. Hikers go right alongside of and to the top of both falls. Early-season hikers should plan to feel lots of water misting onto the trail! The views from the railings at the top of each fall are stupendous. You could also take the John Muir Trail down from Nevada Fall for a loop and fewer crowds. The hike to the Vernal Fall footbridge is 1 mile, with 300 feet of elevation gain. To the top of Vernal Fall it's 1.5 miles, and it's 2.5 miles to the top of Nevada Fall.

YOSEMITE FALLS: A 3.6-mile climb beginning near Camp 4 leads to the very top of Yosemite Falls, where a railing protects visitors while they view the falls from above. This is a steep, rocky, and strenuous climb, but many people make at least part of the trail. Columbia Rock, about one mile up, is a prime destination. The total elevation gain on this hike is 2,600 feet.

HALF DOME: This hike is extremely difficult! Continue past Nevada Fall along the John Muir Trail from Happy Isles, then take the side route that leads, eventually, to the top of Half Dome. On the last part of the climb you will be holding onto cables. It is about 9 miles each way, with 4,800 feet of elevation gain. This is one of the hardest, but most rewarding, hikes anywhere—not for those with a fear of heights. *Due to overcrowding on the cables, permits are required to hike Half Dome. They can be acquired up to four months in advance of the climb.*

THIS IS ONE OF THE **HARDEST,** BUT MOST **REWARDING,** HIKES ANYWHERE—NOT FOR THOSE WITH A **FEAR OF HEIGHTS.**

ONE OF THE BEST HIKES ANYWHERE

AN ACCOUNT FROM HALF DOME HIKER

KIMBERLY ALEXANDER

I hiked to the top of Half Dome during the summer of 2005. The hike up is long and beautiful. It starts out on the Mist Trail, so you pass amazing waterfalls along the way. My hiking partner and I just left early and kept a strong and steady pace. As we approached the back side of Half Dome, there were only occasional views of the massive rock we were going to scale, so it kind of felt like we were sneaking up on it. A few times we caught sight of a line of people moving up the cables. They looked like ants on a boulder. Seeing that from a distance for the first time kind of takes your breath away.

Just before the Half Dome cables was where the work really kicked in. It had already been more than eight miles of steady climbing, and then not only did the trail become steeper, but the higher elevation made it a bit harder for us to catch our breath. Next came the stone steps. This part of the trail took some extra exertion and slowed down our pace some more. I felt exposed as the green and forested trail gave way to the sparseness of rock. But we kept on climbing, until we reached a flatter area below the back side of the dome. All of a sudden we were in the company of the many other hikers who had started up the trail before us. This is also where we got our first close-up view of the cables. Some people were on their way up the ladder-like course and some had just come down. Right below the base of the summit are piles of old gloves. They were there, I was told, not to protect your hands so much as to increase your grip on the cables.

THE VIEW FROM THE TOP OF HALF DOME

I have to admit that once I started climbing, my feelings of exhilaration and excitement were combined with moments of fear. For me it was mostly knowing that what I was now climbing, I would also have to come down. This thought did not ebb as I passed several others on the cables who were descending. Their faces and voices related that they were not too thrilled about being there. Some were even clinging to the cable posts, frozen in fear.

What a feeling when I finally reached the top of the dome, though. There was so much bare granite rock, you couldn't even tell where the drop-off to the face of Half Dome was. There were lots of people strolling about or sitting down for impromptu picnics. After taking in the initial views and a quick recovery from our climb up the cables, we hiked over to the edge. From there I managed to peek over and see the cliff face. The views of the valley and the high country of Yosemite were simply amazing. We stayed up on top of the dome for about an hour. To my great surprise, going down was not at all as troublesome as I thought—I had a blast! Getting back to the valley was a long, slow trek. We took the John Muir Trail from the top of Nevada Fall this time, to make a loop out of it.

I am not sure if I would do it again, but I am so glad I went. One thing I would say to potential Half Dome hikers is go early, and take all the necessary gear: hat, sunscreen, food and water, and extra clothes. Also, just getting to the base of the dome is worth it. Just as sitting in the meadow across from El Capitan and watching the rock climbers is inspiring and fun, so is watching the cables. It's truly a fantastic hike.

BACKPACKING

There are backcountry trails, some simple, some extremely strenuous, throughout the park. Many families with older children do these hikes, which include the High Sierra Trail and the John Muir Trail. An overnight hike is one of the best ways to see Yosemite's wilderness. Inquire at wilderness permit issuing stations for suggested trail routes.

John Muir's Footsteps

Some people say the John Muir Trail is the single best long-distance hiking trail in the country. It starts right in Yosemite Valley at Happy Isles and is one of the routes to the top of Nevada Fall, and also to Half Dome via a side trail. Then it enters Little Yosemite Valley and stays in the wilderness for much of its 211-mile course. The trail passes through, among other places, Tuolumne Meadows, Ansel Adams Wilderness, and Devils Postpile National Monument, and ends at Mt. Whitney, in Sequoia and Kings Canyon National Park. Some people do only parts of the trail, others complete the whole journey, usually in about thirty days. Elevations on the trail range from Yosemite Valley's 4,000 feet to over 13,000 feet. Much of the trail is above 8,000 feet. Most people hike the JMT during the months of July until September because there is snow on a great deal of the path at other times of the year. Permits are required.

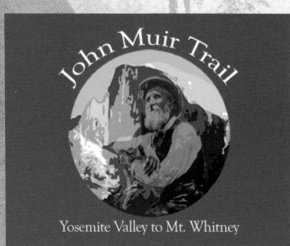

Yosemite Valley to Mt. Whitney

Into the High Sierra

Tuolumne Meadows is the gateway to five fully equipped backcountry camps in Yosemite's wilderness. The camps are on a loop trail and the locations are at Vogelsang, Merced Lake, Sunrise, May Lake, and Glen Aulin, as well as Tuolumne Meadows.

The idea of having accommodations in Yosemite's backcountry with food, water, and canvas tents already set up first came up in 1916. That's when Stephen Mather of the National Park Service asked the concessionaire at the time, the Desmond Company, to build mountain chalets at Tenaya Lake, Tuolumne Meadows, and Merced Lake. The reasons for this were: to reduce crowding in Yosemite Valley by attracting visitors to the high country, to provide a place where visitors could learn about conservation and the National Park Service, and to give people a chance to experience the wilderness without having to carry a lot of supplies. There are now six backcountry sites in Yosemite. The distances from one to the next range from 5.7 to 10 miles, and people can travel on foot or by mule. The camps are extremely popular and it is often necessary to make reservations far in advance.

HIGH SIERRA CAMPS

MAY LAKE

THE BEST OF THE BACKCOUNTRY:
A RECOMMENDATION FROM YOSEMITE PARK RANGER KARI COBB

The whole Vogelsang area—circling by trail, Vogelsang Peak in a loop toward Merced Lake— is my favorite. The peaks are so different there than anywhere else. You walk by them and are constantly wondering, "How was that formed?" There's lots of water out there and river crossings add to the challenge of the terrain but also the scenery. There are also boulder fields, meadows, granite peaks, and canyons with waterfalls. It is so varied, and simply amazing.

GO SEE IT!

A great place to start your high-country Yosemite adventure is the Tuolumne Meadows Visitor Center. This small, rustic facility has displays about wildflowers, butterflies, geology, pinecones, and bears, among other things.

CATHEDRAL PEAK AT TWILIGHT

WILDERNESS SAFETY AND RESCUE

Medical Supplies for the Outdoors

First aid kits are important to bring along for hiking, camping, rock climbing, and backpacking while in Yosemite. They are available through many outdoor suppliers. Some people also make their own. Here are some key items:

First aid manual

Sterile gauze

Adhesive tape

Adhesive bandages in several sizes

Elastic bandage

Antiseptic wipes

Soap

Antibiotic cream (triple antibiotic ointment)

Antiseptic solution (like hydrogen peroxide)

Hydrocortisone cream (1%)

Acetaminophen and ibuprofen

Extra prescription medications (if anyone is taking them)

Tweezers

Sharp scissors

Safety pins

Disposable instant cold packs

Calamine lotion

Alcohol wipes or ethyl alcohol

Thermometer

Plastic gloves (at least 2 pairs)

Flashlight and extra batteries

Mouthpiece for administering CPR (can be obtained from your local Red Cross)

List of emergency phone numbers

Emergency blanket

CALL 9-1-1

If you find yourself in an emergency, the best number to call is the Yosemite Dispatch at 9-1-1 or (209) 379-1992. There is a medical clinic in Yosemite Valley by Yosemite Lodge, on the road that leads to the Ahwahnee Hotel.

YOSAR IN ACTION

AN INTERVIEW WITH YOSEMITE SEARCH AND RESCUE
DOV BOCK

Q: WHAT ARE YOUR PRIMARY DUTIES AT THE PARK?

A: I work within YOSAR (Yosemite Search and Rescue). We provide assistance to park visitors for illness and injury, and to those who get lost on the trail. This is an extremely busy and challenging position! One reason we have so many emergencies is that Yosemite has three to four million visitors a year, and many come in summer. People visit from all over the world to have an outdoor experience, but there are times when it doesn't work out the way they planned. People also come to the park without the needed fitness level, equipment, clothing, or knowledge of how to handle the types of terrain and conditions we have here at Yosemite.

Q: WHERE DO INJURIES TYPICALLY OCCUR?

A: It is when hikers are tired and coming down the trail that problems are more likely. Our most common accident is an injury to the lower leg or ankle area. This part of the body can get tweaked, sprained, or broken from a twist or fall on some of the terrain—which is often caused by not wearing the right kind of footwear. Another all too common emergency is when people are out hiking in strenuous terrain that irritates a medical condition they already had.

Q: HOW CAN INJURED OR SICK PEOPLE GET TO HELP?

YOSEMITE PARK RANGER DOV BOCK

A: People can get help on the trail in a variety of ways. Many trails have a regular flow of hikers, so it is likely that someone will come along and an injured or sick person can report their condition. Some people carry cell phones, and reception is possible in random areas. However, cell phones can't be counted on to work throughout the park, and they won't keep a lost or injured hiker warm through the night. It is best that hikers go out prepared by bringing food and water, a jacket, and a flashlight. Climbers injured or stuck on cliffs often yell, and their voices carry to people below, who then call for help. A few hikers carry beacons that send GPS signals to satellites to alert emergency crews that someone is in trouble.

Q: WHAT DOES YOSAR DO FOR THE HIKER NEEDING ASSISTANCE?

A: Once help arrives, the injured person is first assessed to see if they can hike out on their own with help. If not, then a crew of six to eight people is gathered, along with a litter that has been taken apart and carried on one of the emergency crew members' backs. Once there, the team stabilizes the victim by providing medical care. Then they strap the injured person to the litter and haul them out to a waiting ambulance if needed.

Q: HOW DO YOU PREPARE FOR ALL THE EMERGENCIES AT THE PARK?

A: YOSAR team members go through several types of experiences, or training, that helps with their job. Some YOSARs are medical providers trained at various levels, from basic emergency medical technicians to nurses. We also have technical rope-rescue training, swift-water rescue training, and helicopter-rescue training.

Q: THE HALF DOME CABLES CAN BE DANGEROUS. WHAT EMERGENCY HAS HAPPENED THERE RECENTLY?

A: In the summer of 2009 we had a major rescue on Half Dome that I'll never forget. It was a cold wet day in June and many people were on top of the dome when rain and hail began falling. While scurrying down the suddenly slick cable route, one hiker fell. Others, seeing this, froze on the rock while quickly making rescue calls on cell phones. The fallen hiker, it turned out, had died. Meanwhile, the petrified hikers stayed put and exposed on the cables while the elements continued to pelt them. Eventually, due to the extreme conditions, we had to get rescuers to assist each person down— forty-two in all, a process that took over four hours.

RESCUING AN INJURED CLIMBER FAR
ABOVE YOSEMITE VALLEY

RIDE A BIKE!

Yosemite Valley has thirty miles of mostly flat bike paths through unimaginably beautiful scenery. This activity is extremely popular, so sometimes early mornings or evenings are best, to avoid crowds. Bikes can be rented at Curry Village and at the Yosemite Lodge. Bring locks so you can stop at the many great sites along the way, or even take in a short hike!

LET THE HORSES DO THE WALKING

There are stables in Yosemite Valley near the North Pines Campground. They are open from 7:30 a.m. until 5 p.m. daily, and reservations are highly recommended. Horseback riding is a great way for families to head out onto designated trails. Kids must be at least seven years old. There are two-hour rides and half-day and all-day adventures. Tuolumne Meadows and the Wawona area also have horseback riding.

SADDLING UP IN YOSEMITE VALLEY

A WINTER WONDERLAND

Yosemite gets most of its visitors in summer, but those who come in winter truly get a treat. Bright sunshine often lights up meadows covered in snow and frost, icicles draping over trees, and waterfalls freezing at night and thawing during daylight. There are often glowing sunsets as well.

SNOWBOARDING AT BADGER PASS

There are also plenty of activities, including:

- Cross-country skiing and snow-shoeing—short trips or trips to back-country huts if you're experienced.

- Downhill skiing, snow tubing, and snowboarding at Badger Pass Ski Resort, on the road to Glacier Point.

- The Curry Village outdoor ice rink has been open since the 1930s, and has been ranked as one of the top ten places in the nation to ice skate. Once there you can see why: views of Half Dome, an outdoor fire ring, and smores or hot drinks are all available.

ICE SKATING AT CURRY VILLAGE

RANGER PROGRAMS

Hundreds of Ranger-Led Activities!

Yosemite park rangers and other experts lead hundreds of programs throughout the park for free or a small fee, for visitors of all interest and activity levels, especially in summer. The activities include live theater shows; singing; ranger-led walks and hikes; history programs; art and photography classes; instruction in animal identification, American Indian discoveries, and the geology of cliffs, domes, and waterfalls; stargazing and full-moon walks; wildflower viewing; waterfall viewing; scavenger hunts; sequoia exploring; birding; and bear stories, among many, many more. See the *Yosemite Guide* newspaper for a complete list and for descriptions of all programs and when and where they are offered. Also, evening campfire talks take place throughout the park all summer long. Check local postings for details.

Becoming a Junior Ranger

Every year, thousands of children ages seven to thirteen are sworn in to become Yosemite's next Junior Rangers. This is a great way to learn more about the park and how to take care of it. Here's how you get to become a Junior Ranger: Purchase an inexpensive, self-guided *Junior Ranger Handbook* at any Yosemite visitor center. Complete the booklet, collect a bag of trash, and attend a guided ranger program. Then, rangers will certify your completion of the program and announce your status as a Junior Ranger. Little Cubs is a similar program for younger brothers and sisters, ages three to six.

CAMPING

There are thirteen campgrounds in Yosemite. For seven of them, you can make reservations in advance, and if you are planning to camp in one of these anytime from April through September, you will need a reservation. Yosemite is a popular place! The other campgrounds are on a first-come, first-served basis, and they usually fill up by noon from May through September. Most campsites have water and bathrooms, some take trailers and RVs, and a few have shower facilities nearby.

CAMPING IN YOSEMITE

SENTINEL BRIDGE AND HALF DOME

Yosemite Conservancy is the only philanthropic organization dedicated exclusively to the protection and preservation of Yosemite National Park and enhancement of the visitor experience. The Conservancy works to restore trails and protect wildlife through scientific research and habitat restoration, and offers outdoor programs that provide visitors with unique ways to connect with the park. It has funded over three hundred projects through $60 million in grants in areas including trail and habitat restoration, wildlife protection, education, volunteering, and the production of award-winning books and DVDs. Learn more at www.yosemiteconservancy.org or call 1 (800) 469-7275.

Acknowledgments

I thought I knew Yosemite well when I began this book, but I came to discover that I had much more to learn. As I researched the book, I had the pleasure of meeting many interesting people who would help deepen my knowledge immensely...

First off, I want to thank Kari Cobb and Scott Gediman in the media division of the park for helping me acquire information and set up the interviews. Personally, I want to thank all those I got to speak with regarding the various aspects of Yosemite: besides Kari Cobb and Scott Gediman, they include Dov Bock, Shelton Johnson, Tori Seher, Gus Smith, Christine Loberg, Tom Bopp, Julia Parker, Lee Stetson, Tim Palmer, Ken Yager, Eliza Amstutz, Suzie Gutierrez, Sarah Stock, Linda Eade of the Yosemite Library, and Steve Thompson. You all have added to this book and to my Yosemite knowledge in tremendous ways.

I also owe many thanks to my wife, Kimberley Alexander, who not only provided a story for this book but also has been my biggest supporter in all that I do.

In addition I want to thank Kate Brumage and the rest of the staff at Heyday for all their highly detailed work on this book and for allowing the scope to expand to cover all the topics in here.

Happy Trails!

Mike Graf

Photo Credits

Cover

Clockwise from top left: Eliza Amstutz, photograph by Paul Amstutz, courtesy of the artist. Bear cub © Tony Campbell 2011, used under license from Shutterstock.com. Camping in Yosemite bideriderlondon 2011, used under license from Shutterstock.com.

Bottom cover photograph © Galyna Andrushko, used under license from Shutterstock.com.

Frontispiece

What you can see on your way to the Sentinel Dome © Celso Diniz, used under license from Shutterstock.com.

Welcome to the Best!

A marmot at Olmsted Point © Kippy Spilker 2011, used under license from Shutterstock.com.

Smith Peak © Kippy Spilker 2011, used under license from Shutterstock.com.

Yosemite Falls seen from Cook's Meadow © Steven Collins 2011, used under license from Shutterstock.com.

View of Half Dome from Glacier Point © pmphoto 2011, used under license from Shutterstock.com.

Sequoias in the Mariposa Grove © Steven Castro 2011, used under license from Shutterstock.com.

Along Tioga Road © pixy 2011, used under license from Shutterstock.com.

Tuolumne Meadows © Dean Pennala 2011, used under license from Shutterstock.com.

Hetch Hetchy Reservoir © Thomas Barrat 2011, used under license from Shutterstock.com.

Tioga Road © pixy 2011, used under license from Shutterstock.com.

Yosemite's Rich Past

John Muir, courtesy of the Yosemite NPS Library.

An American Indian house in Yosemite Valley, courtesy of the Yosemite NPS Library.

Julia Parker weaving in Yosemite Valley, 1960, courtesy of the Yosemite NPS Library.

Julia Parker accepting an award at the For All My Relations Conference, 2009: photograph by Dugan Aguilar, courtesy of the artist.

John Muir at Vernal Fall, courtesy of the Yosemite NPS Library.

Teddy Roosevelt and John Muir at Glacier Point, courtesy of the Yosemite NPS Library.

Lee Stetson and Half Dome: photograph by Kenny Krast, courtesy of the artist.

Hetch Hetchy before the dam, courtesy of the Yosemite NPS Library.

O'Shaughnessy Dam at Hetch Hetchy © Better Stock 2011, used under license from Shutterstock.com.

Buffalo Soldiers from the 24th Mounted Infantry, courtesy of the Yosemite NPS Library.

Park Ranger Shelton Johnson in Yosemite: photograph by Ray Santos, courtesy of the artist.

Yosemite Park Ranger Shelton Johnson meets President Obama at the White House: photograph by Pete Souza, courtesy of the artist.

Ansel Adams, courtesy of the Yosemite NPS Library.

Christine Loberg: photograph by Jon Bock, courtesy of the artist.

"Yosemite Fire and Moon": photograph by Christine Loberg, courtesy of the artist.

Postcard featuring the firefall, courtesy of the Yosemite NPS Library.

Wood for the firefall at Glacier Point, courtesy of the Yosemite NPS Library.

Historic entrance to Camp Curry, courtesy of the Yosemite NPS Library.

Tom Bopp entertaining in Yosemite: photograph by Carol Ann Thomas, courtesy of the artist.

It's All about the Rocks

Moonrise over El Capitan © zschnepf 2011, used under license from Shutterstock.com.

Glacial polish and erratics in Tuolumne Meadows: photograph by Chris Falkenstein, courtesy of the artist.

Yosemite's sister park in China, Huangshan: photograph by Ye Shesheng, courtesy of the artist.

Lembert Dome © EARTHaholic 2011, used under license from Shutterstock.com.

Tenaya Lake and Polly Dome © Kenneth Sponsler 2011, used under license from Shutterstock.com.

A lone Jeffrey pine on Sentinel Dome © Tatagatta 2011, used under license from Shutterstock.com.

Hikers ascend Lembert Dome © Steve Kuhn Photography 2011, used under license from Shutterstock.com.

Half Dome © William Silver 2011, used under license from Shutterstock.com.

A rock slide in Yosemite Valley, courtesy of the Yosemite NPS Library.

Tim Palmer: photograph by Ann Vileisis, courtesy of the artist.

Researchers trek across Maclure Glacier: photograph by Tim Palmer, courtesy of the artist.

Researchers explore the Maclure Glacier bergschrund: photograph by Tim Palmer, courtesy of the artist.

Erratic boulders deposited at Olmsted Point by glaciers © pixy 2011, used under license from Shutterstock.com.

Glacial polish in Tuolumne Meadows: photograph by Chris Falkenstein, courtesy of the artist.

The U shape of Yosemite Valley © Jeff Banke 2011, used under license from Shutterstock.com.

The Birth of a Sport

Family climbing at Swan Slab: photograph by Chris Falkenstein, courtesy of the artist.

Mark Wellman and Mike Corbett summiting Half Dome: photograph by Chris Falkenstein, courtesy of the artist.

A climber at the summit © Greg Epperson 2011, used under license from Shutterstock.com.

Camp 4 and the Columbia Boulder: photograph by Chris Falkenstein, courtesy of the artist.

Jules Eichorn, courtesy of Ken Yager.

David Brower, courtesy of The Bancroft Library.

John Salathe and a climbing partner in Yosemite, courtesy of Ken Yager.

Royal Robbins: photograph by Glen Denny, courtesy of the artist.

Warren Harding on the last pitch, ascending El Capitan, 1970: photograph by Glen Denny, courtesy of the artist.

Lynn Hill climbing at Tuolumne Meadows: photograph by Sam Roberts, courtesy of the artist.

Climbers on El Capitan © Greg Epperson 2011, used under license from Shutterstock.com.

Hardware sort-out in Camp 4, 1969: photograph by Glen Denny, courtesy of the artist.

Eliza Amstutz: photograph by Paul Amstutz, courtesy of the artist.

Eliza Amstutz at the top of a climb: photograph by Paul Amstutz, courtesy of the artist.

Eliza Amstutz placing gear on her climb: photograph by Paul Amstutz, courtesy of the artist.

Plants! From Massive to Microscopic

A family hugging a sequoia tree © Juan Camilo Bernal 2011, used under license from Shutterstock.com.

The famous Boole Tree, courtesy of Sequoia National Park.

Stump Meadow, courtesy of Sequoia National Park.

Civilian Conservation Corps workers at the Wawona Tree, courtesy of the Yosemite NPS Library.

Galen Clark's funeral in Yosemite, courtesy of the Yosemite NPS Library.

Galen Clark and friends at the Wawona Tree, courtesy of the Yosemite NPS Library.

The massive Grizzly Giant Tree © Chee-Ong Leong 2011, used under license from Shutterstock.com.

The Bachelor and Three Graces in Mariposa Grove © Chee-Ong Leong 2011, used under license from Shutterstock.com.

A black oak in Yosemite Valley © Mike Norton 2011, used under license from Shutterstock.com.

Dogwood branches over the Merced River © Steven Castro 2011, used under license from Shutterstock.com.

Ponderosa pine bark © Jim Parkin 2011, used under license from Shutterstock.com.

Ponderosa pine forest © Wollertz, used under license from Shutterstock.com.

Beautiful fall colors in Yosemite © Artifan 2011, used under license from Shutterstock.com.

Lichen growing on a tree © Pedro Salaverria 2011, used under license from Shutterstock.com.

A controlled burn in Yosemite, courtesy of the National Park Service.

Yosemite Park Ranger Gus Smith measures a sequoia, courtesy of the National Park Service.

Spring wildflowers in Yosemite © Thomas Barrat 2011, used under license from Shutterstock.com.

Poison oak sign © Ann Baldwin, used under license from Shutterstock.com.

The World's Smartest Bears and Other Fascinating Wildlife

A bear wandering in Yosemite © nialat 2011, used under license from Shutterstock.com.

Yellow-legged frog, courtesy of the National Park Service.

Nighttime view of a Sierra Nevada red fox, photographed with an automatic night monitor, courtesy of the US Forest Service.

Great gray owl: photograph by Joe Medley, courtesy of the artist.

Grizzly bears still roam parts of Montana, Idaho, Washington, Wyoming, Alaska, and western Canada © Shane W. Thompson 2011, used under license from Shutterstock.com.

California ground squirrel © creativex 2011, used under license from Shutterstock.com.

Mule deer © Christopher Testi 2011, used under license from Shutterstock.com.

A family of raccoons eating in the woods © B&T Media Group 2011, used under license from Shutterstock.com.

Big brown bat © Ivan Kuzman 2011, used under license from Shutterstock.com.

Striped skunk © Dennis Donohue 2011, used under license from Shutterstock.com.

A coyote encounters a car © Nelson Hale 2011, used under license from Shutterstock.com.

Mountain lion © Dennis Donohue 2011, used under license from Shutterstock.com.

Bobcat © ben46332011, used under license from Shutterstock.com.

Yellow-bellied marmot © Steve Byland 2011, used under license from Shutterstock.com.

A pika gathers hay © viceralimage 2011, used under license from Shutterstock.com.

Yosemite Park Ranger Steve Thompson, courtesy of the National Park Service.

A black bear in early spring © nialat 2011, used under license from Shutterstock.com.

A bear cub clings to a tree © Tony Campbell 2011, used under license from Shutterstock.com.

A bear breaks into car, courtesy of the National Park Service.

Yosemite Park Ranger Tori Seher, courtesy of the National Park Service.

A bear being tagged, courtesy of the National Park Service.

These signs mark where bears have been hit in Yosemite, courtesy of the National Park Service.

Author Mike Graf and his wife, Kimberly Alexander: photograph by Mark Davis, courtesy of the artist.

Western fence lizard in push-up position: photograph by Joseph V. Higbee, courtesy of the artist.

Western rattlesnake: photograph by Gary Nasif, courtesy of the artist.

American robin © Gregg Williams 2011, used under license from Shutterstock.com.

Acorn woodpecker © Steve Byland 2011, used under license from Shutterstock.com.

Black-headed grosbeak © teekaygee 2011, used under license from Shutterstock.com.

Clark's nutcracker © Steve Bower 2011, used under license from Shutterstock.com.

Common raven © FotoVeto 2011, used under license from Shutterstock.com.

Mountain chickadee © Michael Woodruff 2011, used under license from Shutterstock.com.

Red-tailed hawk © Gregg Williams 2011, used under license from Shutterstock.com.

Steller's jay: photograph by Eric Schaal, courtesy of the artist.

American dipper (water ouzel) © IPK Photography 2011, used under license from Shutterstock.com.

Spotted owl © CHEN WEI SENG 2011, used under license from Shutterstock.com.

Peregrine falcon © Sue Robinson 2011, used under license from Shutterstock.com.

Pileated woodpecker © N. Frey Photography 2011, used under license from Shutterstock.com.

Northern goshawk © Steve Byland 2011, used under license from Shutterstock.com.

Brown-headed cowbird © Doug Lemke 2011, used under license from Shutterstock.com.

Yosemite Park Ranger Sarah Stock, courtesy of the National Park Service.

A curious squirrel © worldsildlifewonders 2011, used under license from Shutterstock.com.

A mountain lion bares its fangs © Dirk Brink 2011, used under license from Shutterstock.com.

Water, Water, Everywhere

Rafting on the Merced River, courtesy of DNC Parks and Resorts at Yosemite.

Upper and Lower Yosemite Falls © EastVillage Images 2011, used under license from Shutterstock.com.

Bridalveil Fall © Tatagatta 2011, used under license from Shutterstock.com.

Vernal Fall from the Mist Trail © ArnaudS2 2011, used under license from Shutterstock.com.

Nevada Fall from the John Muir Trail © Heather L. Jones 2011, used under license from Shutterstock.com.

Horsetail Fall © Dean Pennala 2011, used under license from Shutterstock.com.

Ribbon Fall © Kenneth Rush 2011, used under license from Shutterstock.com.

The top of Chilnualna Falls © Mordy Neuman 2011, used under license from Shutterstock.com.

A moonbow at Yosemite Falls: photograph by Chris Falkenstein, courtesy of the artist.

Horsetail Fall on "fire" © Kenneth Rush 2011, used under license from Shutterstock.com.

Rushing water at the top of Yosemite Falls © Steve Heap 2011, used under license from Shutterstock.com.

A flooded Yosemite campground, 1997, courtesy of the National Park Service.

Yosemite Park Ranger Scott Gediman: photograph by Al Golub, courtesy of the artist.

Highway 140 after 1997 flood damage, courtesy of the National Park Service.

Endless Things to See and Do

Half Dome cable route © Christophe Testi 2011, used under license from Shutterstock.com.

Enjoying the view © Teri and Jackie Soares 2011, used under license from Shutterstock.com.

The view from the top of Half Dome © Mordy Neuman 2011, used under license from Shutterstock.com.

The popular cable route up Half Dome © Mark Yarchoan 2011, used under license from Shutterstock.com.

The John Muir Trail logo, courtesy of Claire Schauer.

About the Author

Mike Graf has been to Yosemite many times and fell in love with it as a child while visiting there with his parents. Mike visits many national parks each year besides Yosemite and has written a national park adventure series for children. The Adventures with the Parkers series includes books set in the Yosemite, Yellowstone, Grand Canyon, Zion/Bryce, Great Smoky Mountains, Olympic, Glacier, Rocky Mountain, Badlands/Rushmore, and Arches/Canyonlands national parks. In addition to writing over seventy books for children and teachers, Mike has been a TV weathercaster, a college lecturer, and an elementary school teacher. You can learn more about Mike Graf by visiting www.mikegrafauthor.com.

THE VIEW FROM OLMSTED POINT

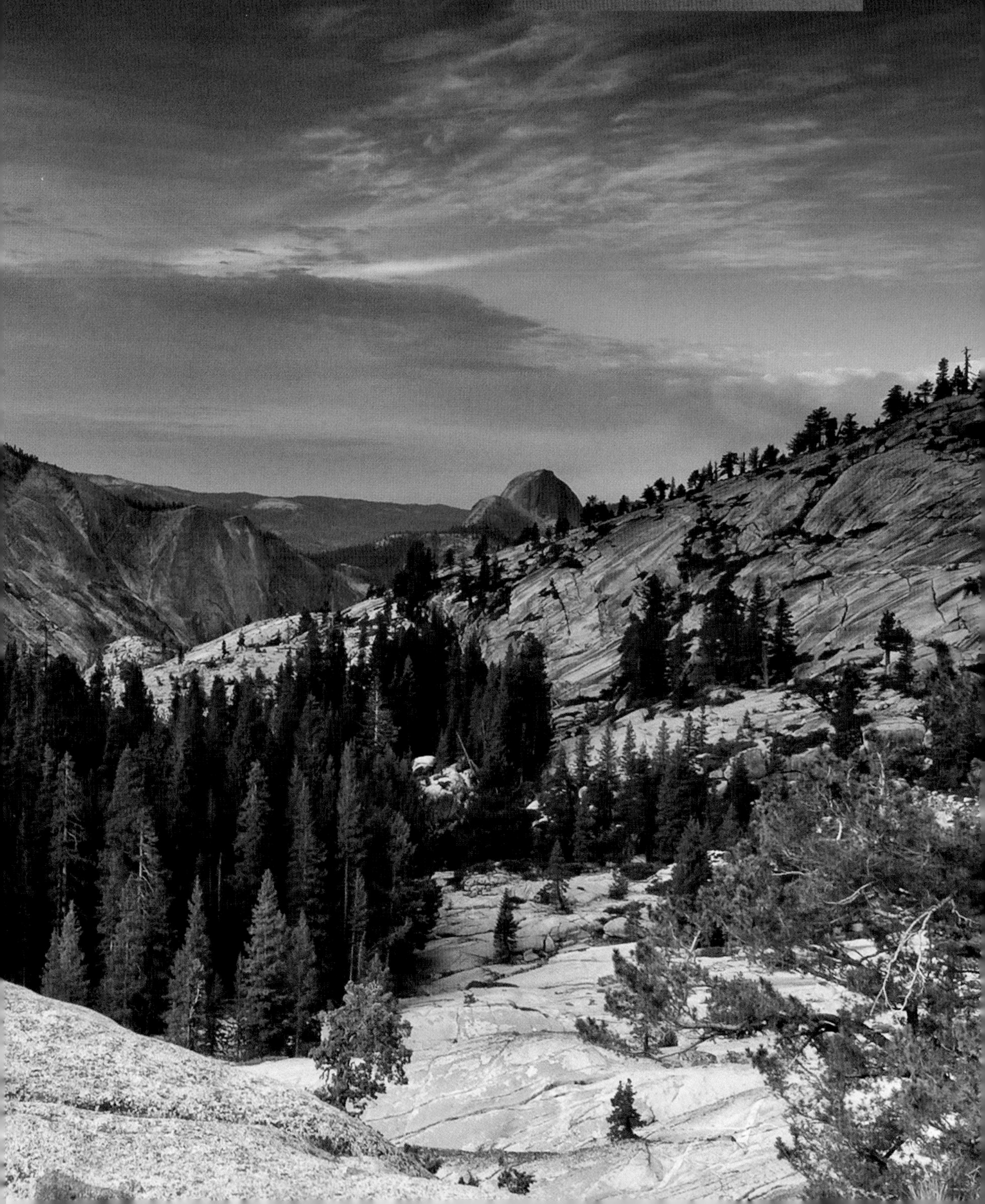